THE VALE OF LANHERNE

James Currah

THE VALE OF LANHERNE

Past and Present

by

Charles Lee
Author of 'The Widow Woman'

Published by
Dyllansow Truran, Cornish Publications
Trewolsta, Trewirgie, Redruth, Kernow.
Telephone (0209) 216796

ISBN No. 0 907566-45-6

Printed by Redborne Printing Works. Redruth.

DEDICATION

To A. C. P. Willyams Esq., J.P., D.L.

In Grateful Acknowledgement of Much Kindness

FOREWORD

This Guide to St. Mawgan was compiled by Charles Lee when he was organist for a year at St. Mawgan Church about 1903. He lived—from the age of about 30—in a delightful cottage which he called Lanvean in what was then deep country in Letchworth Garden City. By that time he had written several books about people of Cornwall which were well received.

His own introductory remarks say it all. He was a remarkable man of his time; rather a square peg in a round hole. A very gentle and modest-natured man, his family and his fellow workers considered him a walking encyclopaedia. He was artistic to his finger tips and an excellent pianist and composer, always more comfortable with his books and piano than with people. He went to work for J. M. Dent, the publishers, as one of their readers. He also became very much involved with amateur events in the Garden City writing words and music for various pantomimes. Gradually as he became older he became almost a recluse but remaining a very gentle, likeable old man, full of knowledge.

The copy, in manuscript form, of the Guide to St. Mawgan was given to his sister who lived with my family at St. Mawgan and on the death of Alice it came into my possession and has lain in a drawer for many years. My friend, Diana Ball, who is herself St. Mawgan born and bred, has encouraged, bullied and made the contacts for getting the manuscript published and I thank her for this.

St. Mawgan is a very different place now to the St. Mawgan of Charles Lee's time, and I am not at all sure he would have approved the changes but that of course is progress.

I should like to thank J. M. Dent the Publishers for allowing me to make use of the photo of Charles Lee, Trevor Hill for the photographs and L. Truran the publisher for thinking this worthwhile.

CONTENTS

Introductory 1

Lanherne 3

The Church 10

The Parish Accounts 31

Carnanton and its Woods 37

The Church-Town and Old Days there 42

The River Valley 51

The Coast and Outlying Parts 55

Footnotes 61

List of Illustrations

James Currah	Frontispiece
View of the Village	19
Lanherne House	19
Mawgan Church & Lychgate	20
The Rectory	20
Falcon Inn, Mawgan	21
St Mawgan Band	21
Mr. Roach & Pupils	22
School Bridge	22
Lawry's Mill, St. Mawgan	23
Staff of Lanherne House	23
Gothic Cross	24
Mawgan Cross	24
Lanherne Cross	25
Pig Sty Cross	25
The Shop at Churchtown	26
Shop Staff	26
Shop at Penport	27
Old Alms Houses	27
Parkin, the Celebrated Cornish Wrestler	28
Stan Beswetherick the Blacksmith	28
Last remnant of Eddyveans Canal	29
Lanvean & Cottage	29
Carnanton Woods, Bridge	30
Mawgan Feast	30

INTRODUCTION

Life in St. Mawgan in Pydar continued almost unchanged from that described by Charles Lee circa 1900 until the 1930s. Until mains electricity was brought to the village in 1935 lighting was still by paraffin lamps, including the street lights; one at the big bridge, the other beside the footbridge. Mains water did not arrive until much later—about 1953. Before that time supplies were pumped to roof tanks or carried from pumps and wells and heated in boilers or on Cornish ranges. The bus service from St. Columb Major to Newquay did not descend into the village but drove along the Southern boundaries past the Carnanton East, Middle and West Lodges to Pale Corner (near Trebelzue) and thence to Newquay. Anyone wishing to travel to this town had to walk up to the road at Mawgan Cross to catch the bus. Eventually in the early 1930s some buses drove down Mawgan Hill and up Long Lane so that even by that date a day out demanded a certain amount of determined effort! For those living on the Northern slopes of the village the walk was much longer and they often chose to walk to St. Columb and back on market days.

St. Mawgan in Pydar has been described, along with similar villages in Cornwall, as a remnant of Victorian times. The school was populated by children whose fathers and grandfathers had attended in their time. Horses were still at work in the fields. The occasional car or motor bike could be heard from afar. All this was due to change swiftly during and after the 1939-45 war.

Some farms had tractors but the implements were usually the ploughs, drills, harrows, binders and wagons of an earlier time fitted with a tractor hitch. This meant that a large workforce was needed on any reasonably sized farm and a positive army was necessary at threshing time, when T. H. Sandry's steam engine would pull a train of machines from farm to farm. It had to make two separate journeys up Long Lane to Lanherne Barton as the hill was too steep to be taken at one go.

Children played cricket and hopscotch and rode their dillies—boxes on old pram chasses– up and down the roads. Many pupils walked, as in previous years, from Mawgan Porth, Trevarrian and Tregurrian, using ancient footpaths and lanes such as Dark Lane and Long Lane. The school bell hanging outside the boys' entrance was rung five minutes before prayers and breathless pupils tore into the playground with seconds to spare.

The old customs still prevailed. Near Christmas the rector provided large baskets of red apples and bags of nuts to be distributed to all and the

Reverend Mother from Lanherne Convent used to send a message inviting the children to go to "The Grove" along Polgreen Lane to gather sweet chestnuts. Only a handful of children took the Scholarship exam, catching the 7.45 a.m. bus to the Grammar School in Newquay, and many girls would become teachers and nurses. Others found jobs in hotels, boarding houses, farms or shops in St. Columb Major or Newquay.

Visitors (not tourists, please note!) were plentiful, returning year after year. They became part of village life joining the locals in the Falcon Inn or helping to shock the corn or build the mows in the harvest fields. The lady artist still sat beside the road sketching the thatched cottage at Lanvean, the church or the bridge near the school.

This life, almost unchanged from that described by Charles Lee, was rapidly transformed after 1938 when markers appeared on the Downs between Longstone on the edge of the Parish and St. Eval Churchtown. St. Eval Aerodrome, which was to play such an important part in World War II, was built shortly afterwards. The farms of Deerpark, Tregonning and Trenoon were incorporated in St. Mawgan airfield. This disrupted the road system on the south of the village rendering it a cul-de-sac with only Ox Lane as a route for buses and lorries, which due to its steep narrow nature, led to some interesting encounters. Mawgan Cross was rescued and placed inside the Churchyard near the lych gate.

Thousands of service personnel, British and American, came to the district in the war years completely disrupting the order of things. Nearly every home with a spare room gave shelter to those people who for reasons of safety or choice lived off the camps. They seemed like people from another world to the parents and children who had seldom, if ever, crossed the Tamar.

After the end of World War II things were never the same again. Tourism flourished and the picturesque village of St. Mawgan was incorporated in the evening coach tours from Newquay and many who first came as tourists returned to live in the area. A housing estate was built in Castle Field on the way up Mawgan Hill, the name confirming a Roman fortification which was excavated before the houses were erected. Similarly a small ancient burial ground was discovered at Lanvean. Nanskivel, the Carnanton Dower-house, was burnt to the ground since the death of Col. E. N. Willyams.

The road communications were reinstated with a new road being cut through the Carnanton Woods to Trebelzue. Many were apprehensive that this road would bring doom to the exposed trees, but it proved a very pleasant approach to the valley. However it meant the acquisition of good farmland and one of the oldest farms in the area—Carloggas—is no more, its large barns and stables flattened and replaced by a suburban type development. The old house stands forlorn in the midst of the new estate.

Similarly Lanvean on the opposite side of the valley has also been fragmented, the farmhouse converted to two houses and the outbuildings to dwellings with the land being sold separately. This is the farm described by Charles Lee.

The Squire no longer casts a benevolent eye over his estate. Carnanton is now run as a large farm and the woods, although still beautiful like others planted about 200 years ago, are showing their age.

The Carmelite convent continues, an important focal point for all Roman Catholics but now containing only thirteen sisters.

The village school thrives but the headmaster no longer lives in the village playing a leading part in its life, and all older children travel daily to the comprehensive schools in Newquay, then follow careers far and wide.

Several landmarks are no more. The huge horse chestnut tree near the convent wall, renowned by successive generations for the quality of its conkers, has gone, also the magnificent sycamore at Lanvean. The huge sycamore by the lych gate, mentioned by Charles Lee, fell, demolishing the Willyams Vault.

Carnanton, or Lawrys Mill, is still there, as idyllic as described by Charles Lee, but now there are no cream teas. The mill at Winsor has gone but the cottages are being converted into a lovely house. The footpath in the field above has gone in its previous raised form but the pleasant walk through the fields to Mawgan Porth endures. The blacksmith emigrated to New Zealand and the smithy became a garage; the ancient door to the forge still hangs there. Butterfields Rectory is in private hands and a nondescript bungalow is sited where once the ancient rectory stood in an Elizabethan garden with box-edged flowerbeds; which existed until a few years ago.

The old families have departed, however, the heart of the village flourishes. The shop opposite the Church, where the Miss Hawkeys were the focus of village life for years, has been well modernised and extended and, even if babies are no longer weighed on the large scales between orders, the friendly service continues. Many cottages have been given a new lease and Long Moor is still the venue on Feast Day even though the serpentine up the hill following St. Mawgan Band is only a distant memory.

Fortunately in a rapidly changing world, the geographical situation of the village defies spoilation and it still meets the description of the beautiful Vale of Lanherne, 80 years after those words were written by Charles Lee.

ACKNOWLEDGEMENTS

P. Wailes for photo by J. Speaight, F.R.P.S. of Stan Beswetherick.
Trevor and Mike for the illustrations.
Redruth Reference Library.
County Record Office.
"This England" for photo of James Currah.

PHYL HELLYAR

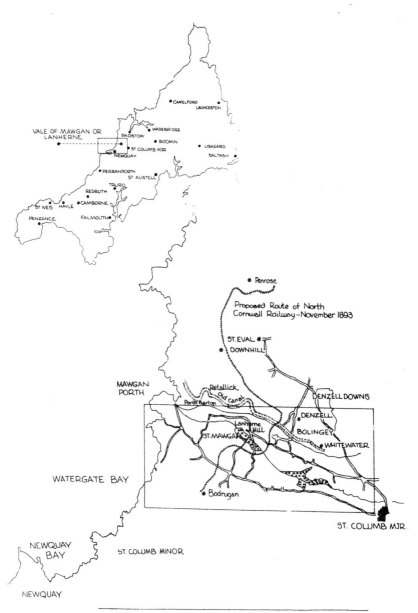

CAMELFORD
LAUNCESTON
VALE OF MAWGAN OR
LANHERNE
WADEBRIDGE
PADSTOW
BODMIN
ST COLUMB MJR
NEWQUAY
LISKEARD
SALTASH
PERRANPORTH
ST AUSTELL
TRURO
REDRUTH
ST IVES   HAYLE   CAMBORNE
PENZANCE   FALMOUTH

Penrose

Proposed Route of North
Cornwall Railway - November 1893

ST. EVAL
DOWNHILL

MAWGAN
PORTH
Retallick
Old canal
Porth Barton
DENZELL DOWNS
DENZELL
Lanherne
MILL
ST. MAWGAN
BOLINGEY
WHITEWATER

WATERGATE BAY

Bodrugan

ST. COLUMB MJR.

NEWQUAY
BAY
ST. COLUMB MINOR

NEWQUAY

𝔙ale of 𝔐awgan or 𝔏anherne

INTRODUCTORY

This little book is inteded chiefly for visitors to the Vale of Lanherne—as a guide on the spot, and as a memento to carry away. By common consent, Mawgan is one of the most beautiful spots in Cornwall—some of us think it the most beautiful spot of all; it is also exceptionally interesting in its associations. This little parish has helped to make history; it has produced warriors, church dignitaries, and conspirators, to say nothing of High Sheriffs and Members of Parliament; within its borders, conceivably, William Noye, the Squire of Carnanton, first meditated that disastrous scheme which brought about the Great Rebellion. Our church presents some remarkable features; we own the two finest ancient crosses in Cornwall; and the silent inaccessible nunnery in our midst affords the visitor a unique opportunity to indulge in romantic fancies or moral reflections, according to taste. The account of Mawgan given in the guide-books is necessarily meagre; the following pages are an attempt to fill it out to respectable plumpness, without letting it run to unprofitable fat.

Some account is also given of the life and ways of Mawgan folk in the past and at the present day, and numerous extracts have been made from our old parish account-books, which, it is hoped, will prove interesting to others besides the casual stranger within our gates.

Mawgan, called Mawgan in Pydar to distinguish it from another Mawgan farther west, is a sea-board parish, situated midway down the north coast of Cornwall. Its 5,468 acres support a population of about 700 souls, mostly engaged in farming. The soil is *shet,* or decomposed clay-slate, fertile in the valleys, barren on the hills. The village is three miles from St. Columb Major, the nearest market town, and six from Newquay. The nearest railway station is St. Columb Road on the Great Western—six miles. Passengers by the South Western can book as near as St. Columb itself, travelling from Wadebridge by the Newquay coach. Mawgan is threatened with a railway station of its own in the near future, a light line having been projected to run from Padstow along the coast to Tregurrian in the south-west corner of the parish, where a large and lonely hotel stand awaiting its advent. Less pretentious accommodation may be had at the Falcon Inn, at several cottages and farm-houses in the village and neighbourhood. Meals are provided at the inn, at Park Eglos Farm in the village, and at Lawrie's Mill in the midst of the woods. Trout-fishing and wild-fowl shooting may be had in their seasons; tickets are issued at the inn. Pedestrians may go freely along the main drives of Carnanton Woods on week-days, and can pass in or out by the upper lodge-gates on presentation of a visiting-card. Bicyclists pay a fee of threepence, and carriage-folk a shilling on each horse. On Sundays, only the lower road to Lawrie's Mill is available, and the by-paths are tabooed to strangers at all times.

LANHERNE HOUSE

For nearly five centuries Lanherne was the principal seat of the Arundells, in their day the wealthiest and most powerful of Cornish families. "The country people," says Carew, "call them The Great Arundells, and greatest stroke, for love, living, and respect, in the country heretofore they bare." At the time of the Domesday survey Roger de Arundell held twenty-eight lordships in Somerset. In the next century several of his descendents possessed lands in Cornwall. At this time Lanherne belonged to the family of one Simon Pincerna, or Butler, who had been cupbearer to Henry II. In the thirteenth century the line of the Pincernas came to an end in an heiress; Sir Renfrey Arundell married her, and established himself at Lanherne. Prolific and enterprising, the Arundells immediately began to spread over the Duchy at a great rate, acquiring land wholesale by marriage and purchase, and establishing branches in all directions, till in Elizabethan days they had no fewer than twelve seats in Cornwall. Their appetite for heiresses was insatiable. It was a common fate for the great Cornish families to end suddenly in an unprofitable crop of girls; and as soon as this happened, one or more Arundells were pretty sure to be found bowing at the young ladies' elbows. In this way they became possessed of the estates of the Le Sores, the Carminows, the Lambournes, and many another vanished name. One of their greatest estates was the manor of Conarton, which was a kind of petty kingship, extending over the whole hundred of Penwith, and exempt from the authority of Crown or Duchy except in matters of life and land. Altogether, at one time or another, the different branches of the family owned some seventy or eighty manors in Cornwall alone, beside great possessions in other parts of the West.

They displayed as much energy in the more active affairs of life as in the peaceful absorption of land. A Sir John of Lanherne was one of Richard II's admirals, and lost his life on an expedition by sea in 1379. Like Clive and other brave men, he was a great dandy. "The said Sir John Arundell," says Hollinshead, "lost not only his life, but all his furniture and apparell for his body, which was very sumptuous, so that it was thought to surmount the apparrell of any king; for he had two and fiftie new sutes of apparell of clothe of golde or tissew, as was reported, all of which together with his horses and geldings, amounting to the valew of ten thousand marks was lost in the see."[1] Another Sir John was retained to serve Henry V at sea with a little army of 1100 men; and his grandson was one of Henry VI's generals in France, and fought afterwards for Queen Margaret at Tewkesbury. In the next century Lanherne can boast of two distinguished rebels. One was Humphrey Arundell, who led the Cornish revolt against the new religious ordinances in 1549;

3

he gathered an army at Bodmin, marched on Exeter, was defeated, taken prisoner, and duly hanged at Holborn. The other was Sir Thomas, brother-in-law of Queen Catherine Howard, and founder of the Wardour branch of the Arundells; he was concerned in the Somerset conspiracy against the Dudleys, and was beheaded in 1552. The last to sally forth from Lanherne in warlike array, was the young Squire John who joined the forces of Charles I at Boconnoc in 1644. He was a mere youth in ward, but the king knighted him, "and that freed his wardship," says one who was present. This was the same Sir John who died in 1701—the last of the old lords of Lanherne.

To the end the Arundells adhered to the Roman church, and from the beginning they took a prominent part in church affairs. They built the Lady Chapel of the church here at Mawgan, and also the fine Arundell Chapel at St Columb. The Sir John who died in 1433 left numerous bequests to the Church: £20 for the St Columb bells, £1 for the restoration of Mawgan Church, £1 for the maintenance of divers lights therein, and £10 for the completion of the tower, with the stipulation that it was to be finished within six years. One of his legacies was curious—£2 to the church of St Piran in the Sands, for honourably and safely enclosing the head of the tinners' patron saint, there enshrined: no unnecessary precaution, perhaps; for there was an active trade in relics, and thieves were abroad. In 1470, a later Sir John gave several timber trees towards the rebuilding of Bodmin Church—a more magnificent gift than it may seem nowadays; wood was then very scarce in Cornwall, and the oak for the pews of the same church had to be fetched all the way from Wales.

At the time of the Reformation the Lanherne Arundells showed signs of wavering in their faith. The Elizabethan Sir John (they were all Sir Johns for three centuries, with the exception of one Sir Thomas), was at first an occasional conformist, but somewhere about 1580 he got under the influence of one Father Cornelius, a Bodmin priest, who led him back to the Roman fold. So important a recusant was not likely to escape the vigilant attention of the Virgin Queen; he was promptly summoned to London to answer for himself, and was kept a close prisoner in Ely Place for nine years. He was released in 1590, but only to die before he could return to Cornwall; his body was brought down with great pomp, and buried in St Columb Church, where there is a brass to his memory and to that of his wife, daughter of an Earl of Derby. The next Sir John was convicted of recusancy in 1606, but James I ordered that he and his estates were to be left unmolested so long as he paid the statutory fine of £20 a month for non-attendance at church.

Several sons of the family entered the Church. Two will be found in

4

the list of the early Rectors of S. Mawgan; but the most distinguished was John, grandson of the Sir John to whom Mawgan owes its beautiful bell-tower. He was educated at a college of Black Monks in St Columb, and began his career in the Church with the family living there. In 1496 he became Bishop of Lichfield, and was translated to Exeter in 1502. "Bishop Arundell", says the Rev. W. S. Lach-Szyrma, "was, it seems, a polite scholar, with much of the sentiment of progress and culture of the Renaissance age. Like most Cornishmen, he was very fond of music, and had excellent choral services in his chapel. He was also, like most Cornish gentlemen of the period, very hospitable and kind to the poor." A notable figure, of whom Mawgan may well be proud. As an Arundell, and a Bishop into the bargain, he had a proper sense of his importance and of the respect due to himself and his cattle. While on a visitation in his Lichfield diocese, he found that his horses were not being supplied with the amount of litter proper for episcopal hackneys. His wrath descended on the unfortunate stablemen, who were made to do penance barefoot, with bundles of straw on their backs.

Mawgan can even boast of a second bishopric—of sorts. One called Bishop (a common name in the parish until recently), shewing promise in his school days, was taken under the protection of the last Sir John Arundell, who sent him to the Roman seminary at Douay. There he took orders, and returned to be house-chaplain at Lanherne, "and from thence", says Hals, "visited and confirmed the Roman Catholics in these parts for many years, by the pretended name of Mr Gifford." Was this the "Roman Catholic bishop in partibus, Bonaventure Gifford," who succeeded Parker as head of Magdalen College in 1688? The same authority tells us that he was consecrated Bishop in the Banqueting House at Whitehall, in the last year of James II. He lived to the great age of 99, and when he died, his heart was taken out and sent to Douay, to be preserved in spirits; but whether this relic of a Mawgan man still remains in its jar there, the present writer knows not.

When the last Sir John died in 1701 Lanherne went to a son-in-law, whose two grand-daughters married, the one a Sir John Gifford, the other the heir of Lord Arundell of Wardour, thus uniting the two branches after a separation of two centuries.[2] The Wardour Arundells have disposed of nearly all their Cornish possessions: the other branches, Trerice, Tolverne and the rest, have decayed and fallen, and now of all those vast estates there remain only a few acres here in Mawgan that still own an Arundell for their lord. "Reader, go thy way," says an eighteenth century divine, improving the occasion, "secure thy name in the book of life, where the page fails not, nor the title alters nor expires; leave the rest to Heralds and the Parish Register."

What kind of life did they lead at Lanherne in the old days? Carew gives us a notion in his sketch of the Cornish gentry of Elizabethan times:

"They keep liberal, but not costly builded or furnished homes; give kind entertainment to strangers; make even at the year's end with the profits of their living; live void of factions among themselves . . . and delight not in bravery of apparel; yet the women be very loth to come behind the fashion, in new-fangledness of the manner, if not in costliness of the matter, which perhaps might over-empty their husbands' purses. They converse familiarly together, and often visit one another. A gentleman and his wife will ride to make merry with his next neighbour; and after a day or twain, those two couples go to a third; in which progress they increase like snowballs, till through their burdensome weight they break again."

The Arundells were particularly famous for their hospitality, which sometimes, we are told, "out went all show of competence"; and what Cornish hospitality was like, even so late as the eighteenth century, we can judge by the style in which the last Lord Radnor kept house at Lanhydrock, where a bullock was killed every week, a sheep every day, and every morning whatever remained over of meat, bread, and the daily allowance of beer, was distributed at the gates: with anything but the best effect on the thrift and morals of the neighbourhood. In the sixteenth century, John Carminow of Fentongollan kept open house from Christmas to Twelfth Night, and his ordinary allowance for the period was 12 bullocks, 60 bushels of wheat, and 36 sheep, "with hogs, lambs and fowls of all sorts, and drink made of wheat and oat malt proportionable."

The older part of Lanherne House dates from 1580, and is a charming specimen of the local architecture of the time—picturesque, dignified, and unpretending, with mullioned windows and an arched doorway of Catacleuse stone. The waterpipes, instead of being hidden round a corner, are made the most of with elaborate mouldings, so as to give just a sufficient touch of ornament to the plain front. Some of the stone-work is carved with scallop-shells, and with the wolf—the Arundell crest ever since one of the first of the race married the heiress of Trembleth— "Wolf's Town"—in St Ervan. The rest of the building is of more modern date, but well in keeping. Somewhere in the house there is said to be a secret chamber, in which a priest lay hid in the days of the Elizabethan persecution.

As everybody knows, Lanherne is now occupied by a community of Teresan nuns, who fled to Britain from Antwerp at the time of the French invasion in 1794, and had the place (then in a ruinous state) as a gift from the eighth Baron Arundell of Wardour. The order is a reformed branch of the Carmelites—Barefooted Carmelites they are sometimes called, but more properly *Discalced,* from that wearing heel-less shoes. They lead the strictest lives, never touching animal food, never leaving the convent walls, and never seeing a man face to face except when the doctor is called in at the last necessity. They take their recreation in the two walled-in gardens, which are connected by an underground passage; and from the high ground about the nunnery a glimpse may occasionally be caught of dark-robed figures walking quickly to and fro, or stooping over a flower-bed. It is a tempting subject to moralise on—this enclosure of bleak austerity in the sweetest-smiling valley of the West: but from what one hears, the Nuns' lives are not without their amenities, and their liberal chatities keep them in touch with the little world outside. At one time—a century ago—their confine-ment was nothing like so rigorous. A dwarf fence surrounded the gardens that are now shut in with high walls; friends in the neighbourhood paid visits and conversed with the sisters; and when a nun died, the com-munity went in procession to the church, where the body was buried in the Lady Chapel according to the rites of the Church of England. But once a terrible thing happened. The story is told in *The Autobiography of a Cornish Rector.* A neighbouring family had brought some friends to see the nuns.

> "They were in the midst of a merry gossip, the old gentleman exchanging pinches of snuff with Sister Mary Joseph, and the ladies admiring their little specimens of filigree and embroidery; when all at once, without a word or gesture that could excite suspicion, one of the strangers, a sturdy young ruffian of five-and-twenty, rushed across the room, and seizing the youngest and prettiest of the sisters round the waist, gave her a loud smacking kiss."

The scene of confusion and dismay that followed can be imagined. Profuse apologies were offered, and the offender was ignominiously dismissed from the neighbourhood; but from that hour the nuns were dead to the world. The present high wall rose round the garden; a cemetery was plotted out within the enclosure, and the windows of a house hard by that overlooked the convent were blocked up.

The Convent chapel was formerly shown to visitors, but the un-mannerly behaviour of some cheap trippers has caused this privilege to be taken away of late, though strangers may still attend the services. The altar-picture is attributed to Rubens—and a very disagreeable picture it is; the vestments are of antique Flemish embroidery, and are said to be the finest of the kind in Europe. There is a tradition that the services of the Roman Church have been celebrated here uninterruptedly since pre-Reformation days.

The fine old red-brick garden wall is worthy of notice. The noble Spur Valerian, with its grey-green leaves and thick heads of ruddy pink blossoms, grows in profusion along the top, and the Evergreen Alkanet clusters about the base: a notable plant, for its flowers of heavenly blue, for its high-sounding Arabic name, and for the fact that it is one of those herbs which have the good taste to prefer Cornwall as a home before all other parts.

In the nuns' burying-ground, which is on the side of the convent nearest the church, stands the finest ancient decorated cross in Cornwall. It does not really belong to Mawgan at all, but was removed here long ago from Roseworthy in Gwinear, the former seat of the present possessors of Carnanton. Its fine state of preservation—the carvings as clear as when they were first cut—is due to its being made of Pentewan stone, which is at once more durable and more tractable than the granite of which most Cornish crosses are fashioned. Most of these ornamented crosses set up in churchyards for devotional purposes, but this one, from the inscription upon it, appears to be commemorative. Antiquaries decipher on the front the names of *The Blessed Eid and Imah,* and on the back *Runhol,* probably the name of the man who set it up. On the upper part of the front is a figure of Christ, clad in a tunic. The right side of the shaft is filled with the figure of a dragon, its head at the bottom, and its serpentine body twining up and down again in a continuous figure of what is known as Stafford Knotwork, and terminating in the animal's mouth. There is only one other specimen of this "zoomorphic interlaced work" in Cornwall, and that is on a cross at Sancreed, which appears to have the same name, *Runhol,* upon it. It is an easy conjecture that the two crosses were erected by the same man. The date is approximately fixed by the style of the ornament—"a local variety of the Lombards-Byzantine style"—at somewhere between 600 and 900 A.D.

There are two other ancient crosses in Mawgan, beside the Gothic cross in the churchyard. One, which is deposited in the church, was removed here in 1903 from Bodrean near Truro, where it was found built into the wall of a pig-stye. Mr Arthur T. Langdon, F.S.A., in his book on Cornish crosses, gives a long list of equally odd and inappropriate purposes to which these ancient monuments have been applied by farmers, and by others who had not the farmers' excuse of ignorance. In 1896, when Mr Langdon's book appeared, many were still being used as gate-posts, stepping-styles, foot-bridges, Ordnance bench-marks, and rubbing-stones for cattle.

The other gives a name to Mawgan Cross, a hamlet about a mile from the Churchtown on the road to St Columb and Newquay. It stands in the hedge at the cross-roads, and has upon it a rude figure of our Lord with uplifted arms—Latin crosses of this form, with the arms tilted upwards, being peculiar to Cornwall. Such wayside crosses were erected as praying stations, or "to guard and guide the way to the church", or for both purposes. Their original position was probably in the middle of the road, and dead bodies were set down by them while the bearers rested and recited prayers. The name of another hamlet on the opposite side—Trevena Cross—points to the former existence here of a second cross of this kind, but all trace and memory of it has vanished.

THE CHURCH

Our Church stands immediately below the part of Lanherne House which is occupied by the nuns; and, in spite of the high wall that now rises between, it still has the air of an appendage to the convent—a circumstance which arouses the surprise and disgust of some of our sturdy Methodist visitors, to whom the mere physical proximity of "Popery" is corrupting. But it is to its long and close connection with the Manor House that the Church owes its chief beauties, within and without.

It will be noted that the tall and singularly graceful tower is on the south side, and not in its more usual position at the west end. "The tower at the side of the nave," we are told, "was erected by a lord of the manor, and the western tower by the parishioners"; and the two upper stories of our tower, as we know, were built between 1433 and 1439, out of a legacy of £10 bequeathed by Sir John Arundell.

Probably there was once another church on the site, of which the Norman bowl of the font may be a relic. Originally—in 1279—the plan of the church was cruciform—nave, chancel and two transepts. A century later, the Arundells built the Lady Chapel, thus filling in the upper right-hand angle of the cross. Then, in the fifteenth century, a time of great activity when most Cornish churches were added to, the South Transept was merged into a new South Aisle. The beams of the wagon-roof were "restored" away when Mr Butterfield was let loose on the church in 1850, but most of the original wood-work still does duty in the North Transept, and some fragments of it, together with the curiously carved bosses or rosettes, remain in the porch.

Immediately opposite the main entrance is another door. These north doors were popularly called the Devil's doors, and were left open during baptisms, to give the Prince of Darkness an opportunity of escaping homewards to his region of gloom and thick-ribbed ice. But there is a stone over our door outside, inscribed with the date 1701 and the initials I.D., W.E. (John Dennis, William Ellery, churchwardens for the year), which seem to indicate that it is a comparatively modern convenience for the use of more respectable folk.

A hagioscope, or squint, pierces the wall between the Chancel and the North Transept, so arranged that those sitting where the organ now is could command a view of the Altar. Close by, a piscina marks the position of a former subsidiary altar.

The Rood Screen, gaily coloured in red, green and bice, picked out with gold—dates, according to Mr Sedding, from the end of the sixteenth century. In the middle, above the fan-tracery that rises out of the pillars, two angels support a shield bearing the six swallows of the Arundell arms, quartered with a *bend,* the device of the Carminow family. On the other side is a carved decoration of large vine leaves and grape-bunches. Once this screen extended right across the front of the Lady Chapel; the name of the man who mutilated it within the last century is buried in merciful oblivion.

Fixed to the screen on the chancel side is a fragment of a much older screen; a long narrow strip of dark oak, deeply carved with a most intricate design of men and animals in a thicket of vine-branches. The carving is not easy to make out from below, and the visitor may have to take some of the following details on trust. These are the figures, taken from left to right:

(1) Four birds, one above another, peering into the thicket with outstretched necks.

(2) Facing them, an animal of very doubtful species.

(3) A bird resting on the upper boughs of the thicket.

(4) A maned beast, probably a lion, facing towards the night. Its face like some of the others, has been planed down to blankness.

(5) Two figures—perhaps a man and a demon—crouching face to face in bellicose attitudes, and holding in their hands weapons which they are about to cast at each other.

(6) Several grotesque birds with small bodies, long thick necks, and big crested heads, craning towards the next figure.

(7) A beast rampant, its hind legs on a bough, its forelegs lifted; about to spring on the birds.

(8) An ape-like creature sitting upright and playing on a pipe. It faces to the right, nearly touching the next figure.

(10) A large beast, which in the present state of the fragments appears to have had enough of sylvan adventures, and is hurriedly quitting the thicket.

The thicket is the Church, the True Vine, under whose branches all creatures, clean and unclean, find shelter. The birds are spirits, generally good spirits; the beasts are demons, shewn here in conflict with the birds; but the lion typifies the Redeemer—the Lion of Judah. We know that in many cases our old churches were built and decorated by local artificers; thus in 1491 Matthy More, a carpenter, contracted to do all the woodwork of Bodmin Church for the sum of £92; and it is pleasant to think that it was probably the Mawgan master-carpenter of the period who thus let his fancy wander and play through the intricacies of this slip of oak. There is another piece of old carving though not so old—running along the backs of the chancel seats on the south side. Here again we find the symbolical vine-leaves, joined two by two to a bit of twig.

Forty-one of the old oak bench-ends remain, ranging in date from the fourteenth to the sixteenth century, and carved in bold relief on their seventy-seven standards with all manner of devices. About half are of ecclesiastical import: such are the Lantern, Ladder, and Pincers; the Scourge, which occurs four times; the Three Nails (two for the hands and one for the crossed feet, according to the ancient tradition); the Column, the Crown of Thorns, the Spear, and the Sponge—all having reference to the Passion. Then we have different forms of the Sacred Monogram; the Fleur-de-lys and the crowned M of the Virgin; and three that have reference to S. Peter—the Cock that reproved him, the Fish from whose mouth he took the tribute money, and his Sword, with Malchus' *left* ear attached to it. Others are the devices of families that once worshipped here; midway down the north aisle occur three curious figures—a kind of pan-pipes, known to heralds as *Clarions* or *Organ-rests*—the arms of the famous family of Grenville, whose heiress married an Arundell; at the top, near the organ, comes T.A., which may stand for Thomas Arundell; and at the bottom, below the north door, is an eagle preening its feathers, the device of the Rous family.[3] Others again seem to be merely fanciful ornaments, and some baffle conjecture. One can understand the dragon—the Old Enemy writhing in agony within the sacred precincts; but what is the extraordinary creature with protruding tongue, the head of a hippopotamus, and the body of any animal you like to mention, which occurs three times? All we can say is that the nightmare zoology of the heralds contains no uglier beast. Can it be the Wolf of Trembleth? Wolves were not extinct in Cornwall when it was first carved here. The artist might have done better. The pulpit, of black oak, is said to date from Marian times. On five panels we find again the symbols of the Passion: on the first the Column, Cords, and Scourge; on the second the Nails; on the third the pierced Heart resting in a chalice, with the pierced Hand and Feet arranged about it; on the fourth the Crown of Thorns hung on the Cross, with I and M on either side, a royal Crown below, and below that again a Rose; and on the fifth the Sponge on the end of a reed.

Such is the Book of Mawgan Church—an epitome of history, doctrine and genealogy, cut on wood by unlettered men for their unlettered brothers to read.

On the floor of the chancel is an early fifteenth-century brass with the figure of a tonsured priest, conjectured to be the William Trebelle who was rector here from 1411 to 1415. In the Lady Chapel are three other brasses, one depicting a lady in Elizabethan attire (said to be

Cyssel, daughter of Sir John Arundell who died in 1590), the second a gentleman in armour—George, Cyssel's brother—and his wife, whose name was Isabel; and the third another gentleman with a mild dreamy face and a rich, long-sleeved robe—perhaps the Edward Arundell who died in 1587. On the screen which parts the Sanctuary from the Lady Chapel are fixed a number of coats of arms and poetical inscriptions, all referring to members of the Arundell family. Twelve small shields on the Sanctuary side set forth their pedigree in what is now an unknown language to most; and on the other side is the shield of the Sir John mentioned above, with the Trembleth wolf surrounding it. A strip of brass running along the screen is made up of two portions incorrectly joined. The first reads *Here under lyeth buryed Jane Arundell,* but the rest of the inscription, together with a poetical acrostic which was attached to it, has disappeared of late years—removed to the nunnery, it is said. Jane died unmarried in 1577, and during her life-time, according to the vanished inscription, she served five queens. Presumably we must include in the total three of Henry VIII's short-lived spouses, which hardly seems fair counting. The rest of the strip refers to Elizabeth, Jane's sister-in-law, "wyf of John Arundell Knyght, a daughter of Ge[r]arde Dannet Esquire one of the pryve Counsell of our late Kynge of famos [memory]."

Below are five poetical inscriptions in memory of various Arundells. One of them is to Cyssel or Cecilia aforesaid.

"Not shee ye saynt, whose name thou beare, and vertuos lyfe embrace,
But Arundell, the same I meane, that syrved Quene Marys grace."

Another commemorates Mary Arundell, one of Cecilia's sisters, a maiden lady of "twise twenty yeares." Another, to their brother Edward, is an ingenious perversion of the story of the Judgement of Paris, turned to account for the glorification of the Arundells in general and the dead man in particular. "Three mightie monarchs of renowne," *Nature, Fortune,* and *Grace,* are represented as contending for his favour, "ech seeking other to surmount and acquyre souverance." Dame Nature begins by heaping on him

"such treasures as in one to fynd is rare,
A wyt profound that well might mach the sages sevne of olde,
A parsonage such as gracious was and goodly to beholde."

"Famous Fortune" comes next, with "lands and livings" in her hand. You are bidden to note that

"Of brethren five though youngest he were, to lyve yet had he well,
His worthy house him worshipp gave, so famous ys that race,
The family of **Arundels,** well known in every place."

And lastly, Grace, not to be outdone,

"gave him a godly end,

A gyft wherbi his soule ys sure to glory to assende.

Where unto **Grace** and **God** he yealds the price and prayse for aye,

What **Fortune** or dame **Nature** gave **Death** having tane away."

In homely phrase, they thought no small bones of themselves, these Aru ndells.

On the wall hard by is a large slate slab which records the burial beneath of Humphrey, son and ultimate heir of Attorney-General Noye. The date is 1679; the chapel which the Arundells built, and in which they had worshipped for three centuries, had now become an appanage of the other great house. Mr John Oliver Wyllyams, head of the "Antient and Respectable Family" of Carnanton, also lies buried here, and there is a marble memorial to the late Mrs Brydges Williams, a daughter of the Levy family, and sister to Sir Edward Lawson.

There are two ancient coats of arms on the West Wall. One is that of the Vyell family, described in the terrific jargon of heraldry as *Argent, a fesse raguly gules between three ogresses*; but when you look for the ogresses, they dwindle down into little round buttons. It probably commemorates Dorothy Vyell of Trevorder in St Breock, who married George Arundell in 1608. She was one of six sisters, among whom the family estate was divided in default of a male heir. A memorial slab in St Breock Church gives a list of them and their husbands, and draws the melancholy moral:

"Things that be ecciding excelent
Be not comenli longe permanent."

The other coat, which still retains the colours of its ancient emblazoning, bears as a crest the three covered cups of the Pincerna family, and displays the arms of Coleshill (a goat), and others. The Arundell and Coleshill families were connected by Joan, sister of Sir John Coleshill (who was twenty-three when he was slain at Agincourt). She married Sir Renfrey Arundell, and became the mother of John, Bishop of Exeter.

The other memorials in the church call for little remark. One slate slab, which was originally place in the belfry floor, is adorned with forbidding full-length portraits of Henry and Dorothy Stephen in Jacobean costumes.

On the Vestry door is placed an ancient iron crucifix which was found fastened in the wall of a farm-house near Cubert. The Vestry itself is a modern addition.[4] Of the old box which now stands there, and of what it contains, some account will be found farther on. The parish registers go back to 1683.

By the North Door hangs a list of the Rectors of the church, complete from 1279, the year of the dedication, when one William de Aldesworthe was installed. It includes some interesting names. The third Rector, Benedict de Arundelle, left Mawgan in 1313 to become the third provost of Glasney College, lately founded by Bishop Bronescombe: to become famous later as the chief seat of Cornish learning. Succeeding incumbents bear names of well-born ancient Cornish families; in 1313 we have Ralph de Pridiaus or Prideaux of the Padstow family; in 1336 Robert de Umfrevyle (an Umphraville married Alice of Lanherne, widow of the first Arundell who came here, and held Lanherne by her right in 1302); and in 1446 David Cusworth, or Cosowarth, one of an old and notable family of the neighbouring parish of Colan. Three rectors held the living in the seven years between 1410 and 1416; those were the days of the great Bishop Stafford of Exeter, who, like Wesley, believed in continually shifting his ministers from one district to another. St Columb Major had ten rectors during the twenty-four years of his rule.

The last Rector before the Commonwealth bore the remarkable and most unclerical name of Hannibal Gammon. He was a Presbyterian, and became chaplain to the Roundhead Lord Robartes at Lanhydrock, where he helped to gather a large library of divinity, and where also, it is odd to note, he must have been intimately acquainted with the last of the Cornish ogres—that terrible Tregeagle, who in life was steward at Lanhydrock, and whose morbid posthumous activity, in weaving ropes of sand and baling out lakes with limpet shells, has not ceased to this day. Gammon's Puritan leanings did not save him from being deprived of his living, perhaps at the time his patron fell out with Cromwell. He published some sermons while at Mawgan. The title of one, preached when the quarrel between King of Parliament was beginning to simmer, sounds a warlike note:

"God's Smiling to Amendment, or Revengement, with Preservatives against Revolting. In a Sermon preached at the Assizes, in Laun-ceston, the 6. of August, 1628. By H. Gamon, Minister of God's Word, at S. Mawgan, in Cornwall."

The Rev. Thomas Pendarves was a relative of the William Arundell of Mendarva who presented him to the living in 1683. His son William, born at Mawgan in 1690, was knighted by Queen Anne, married a daughter of Sidney Godolphin, and represented St Ives in the Parliament of 1713. Three of the name of John Tregenna held the living in three generations. They belonged to a younger branch of the St Ives Tregennas, who had settled at Polgreen (now a farmhouse) in this parish. A daughter of the last of the three married Whitaker, the Historian of Manchester and Cornwall, the Vindicator of Mary Queen of Scots, the Ascertainer of Hannibal's True Course over the Alps, and a voluminous writer on fifty subjects besides: "the most justly celebrated Whitaker," one fellow antiquarian calls him: "that blockhead Whitaker," says another.

Richard Paul, Rector in 1804-5, had a son, the Rev. Robert Bateman Paul, who was an Archdeacon of the Church in New Zealand and a Prebendary of London, and was the author, under the pseudonym of James Hamley Tregenna, of an entertaining book, *The Autobiography of a Cornish Rector,* the earlier chapters of which contain an interesting picture of life in Mawgan—or "St Vallery" as he calls it—a century ago.

Lastly, Thomas Sutton was inducted here at the age of eighty-six, which surely constitutes a record, even for the easy-going Georgian days.

In 1294 the benefice was worth £6.13s.4d., in 1521 £26.13s. 4d., and in 1831 £585.

The musicians' gallery used to be at the west end of the south aisle, hiding the beautiful tracery of the fourteenth century window there. Here sat the singers, and a band consisting of two flutes, two clarinets, or a clarionet and cornet, and one or two "bass-viols". When the parson said, "Let us sing to the praise," etc., and gave out the first verse of the psalm, then the clarionet piped the keynote, the bass-viol scraped out the four notes of the common chord from top to bottom, and away went voices and instruments in full cry through Dowland's *Old Common* or Ravenscroft's *Salisbury,* or some other ancient and dignified melody, to the words of Tate and Brady.[5] When the clarionet "cowked", or squeaked, as clarionets will for lack of moisture, the player would stamp down from the gallery, and go and dip his reed in the river outside. They were an independent and impartial band; for many years certain of them regularly began Sunday by attending the Convent service, and supplying what music was required there; afterwards crossing over to the later service in the Church.

In the parish books at the beginning of the last century there are several entries referring to the musicians, e.g.:

"Pd. Thos Dungey for the Singing for the Year — £1.11s.6d."

(Annually till 1807).

"Pd. the Expences for a Treat to the Singers — £1.12s.11d."

"Pd. Wm Cayzer for Reeds for the Instrument — 7s."

"Pd. for a Singing Book for Ralph — 2s.6d."

The inevitable end came about fifty years ago, when musicians and gallery were done away with, and a harmonium was substituted. One of the flautists is still (1903) living in the parish.

Three of the six bells in the tower are of ancient date; the oldest (the tenor) was cast in 1640. "Kettle, crock, and pan," they were rudely

16

styled by the old folk. The ringers had plenty of prerequisites in former days. Even at a pauper's funeral they got their shilling in cash or drink, and on occasions of public rejoicings they were liberally fed for their services. In 1715 we have

"Pd. the ringers the Crownation day — 2s.6d."
"Pd. the ringers on ye Accession to ye Crown — 5s."

And again in 1761,

"Pd. the ringers the Kings Crown Nashon day — £1."
"Pd. the ringers when wee took Quebek — 6s."

For years a colony of hive bees has been established within the walls of the North Transept. There are crevices in the stones outside which admit them to some hollow interior space, supposed to be filled with hundredweights of inaccessible honeycomb. Since the removal of the organ to this side of the church, they have had the deep pedal pipes for neighbours; and one wonders what they make of the gigantic hummings of the sixteen-foot C. If bees are capable of religious awe, they must feel it when this tremendous, super-apian voice awakes.

As for St Mawgan himself, we learn that he was one of a family of hereditary bards. His father was court poet to the king of Ireland, and did much to help St Patrick in his work of conversion. Somewhere about 468, Mawgan went to Wales and there set up a School for Saints, where St David and Paulinus received their training. It is not likely that he ever visited our parish, which in the older records is styled, not Mawgan, but Lanherne. When Rome grew powerful in the Church, people seem to have been seized with doubts whether these obscure Celtic saints, unplaced as they were in the Roman calendar, had power to protect them properly; so they proceeded to put themselves under the wing of some saint of acknowledged status. In our case the popular, poor man's Saint— Nicholas—was judiciously chosen. Later still, St Mawgan was disowned altogether, and the dedication informally transferred to St James, whose festival happens to fall on the same day—July 25th. The present Rector has righted this matter again, and restored the neglected Saint to his dues.

In the church-yard, outside and above the porch, stands what is probably the best specimen in Cornwall of a sculptured Gothic Cross. It has escaped with little injury from the fury of the iconoclasts, and does not seem to have been removed since its erection six hundred years ago. It is of the lantern-headed type, and stands five feet high on a slender octagonal shaft. In its four canopied niches are some rudely sculptured figures, about the meaning of which some wild guesses have been made. The group on the western side, according to the most probable inter- pretation, represents the Annunciation. The crowned Virgin kneels before a lectern, and by her side stands a crowned figure, intended for the Third Person of the Trinity. A scroll, which may once have borne the words of the Salutation, issues from its mouth, twines round a pillar, and is held at the other end by an angel who is seated on a block in the corner. The Lysons brothers thought that the group represented some ancient legend of a king and queen; the scroll they took for a serpent biting the king's face. On the opposite side, the Father, represented as an old bearded king, holds upon His knees the crucified Son. The other two niches contain figures of mitred bishops with their pastoral staves.

Close by, is the grave of ten men who drifted ashore in a boat at Beacon Cove, frozen to death, on December 15th 1846. The stern of their boat did duty as a head-piece to the grave until lately, when it was replaced by a piece of wood cut into a similar shape. A few old folk can remember this tragedy, and recall how impressive the procession to the churchyard was; for the snow lay deep on the ground, so that the footsteps of the assistants and the wheels of the cart that carried the bodies made no sound, but came on in dead silence.

A fine sycamore stands in the church-yard near the gate. Growing apparently wild over some of the graves will be found that handsome hawkweed with deep orange blossoms, which north-country folk call Grim-the-Collier because of the black hairs that clothe its stem.

View of the Village

Lanherne House

19

Mawgan Church & Lychgate

The Rectory

St Mawgan Band

Falcon Inn, Mawgan

21

Mr. Roach & Pupils

School Bridge

Lawrey's Mill, Mawgan

Staff of Lanherne House

23

Gothic Cross

Mawgan Cross

24

Lanherne Cross

Pig Sty Cross

The Shop at Churchtown

Shop Staff

26

Shop at Penport

Old Alms Houses

27

Parkin, the Celebrated Cornish Wrestler

Stan Beswetherick the Blacksmith

Last remnant of Eddyveans Canal

Lanvean & Cottage

Carnanton Woods, Bridge

Mawgan Feast

THE PARISH ACCOUNTS

In the Vestry of Mawgan Church stands an old deal box, for the making of which Richard Leywarne was paid three shillings in 1703. It contains a number of books and papers, namely: A book of the overseers' accounts from 1681 to 1765; another book of the same from 1797 to 1813; the road surveyors' account-book from 1807 to 1836; about a hundred indentures of parish apprentices, the earliest dated 1731, the latest 1829; eighteen bonds for the maintenance of children—the earliest of these, dated 1623, is the oldest document in the box; and a number of miscellaneous bills, notices, examinations, etc.

The first and most abiding impression made by an examination of these documents is one of astonishment at the multifarious duties that fell on the shoulders of those who had the care of the poor in those days. There is usually an annual charge of three shillings "for writing our book and keeping our Account," and the scribe fairly earned his fee. In an average year there will be as many as a hundred separate entries. Everything is put down—so much allowance per week to this pauper, so many gifts of food, money, or fuel to that; particulars of the making and repairing of every garment; all the burial fees, to parson, clerk, watchers, layers-out and ringers; doctors' bills, workmen's wages, building materials, and fifty other matters, each with a line to itself. Take a specimen year at random—1682-3 from Easter to Easter.

Six old folk—the permanent paupers of the parish—John Peeter, Sara Petrick, Enegoe (Inigo) Moyle, Florence Vanson, Ed: Dankester, and John Orton, (what capital names!) get their weekly dole of a shilling or fourteen pence for the fifty-two weeks, and forty-two sums varying from sixpence to three and sixpence are given to others by way of occasional relief. "Washing Enegoes clothes," a ceremony which takes place once a year, costs the parish two shillings, and "a paire of Linings" for the same old gentlemen come to 1s.10d. Twelve new pair of shoes are provided at an average price of half a crown, and four old pair are cobbled for ten-pence a pair. Five shirts and five smocks cost about three shillings each. John Orton has a new pair of stockings given him, and his old ones are "vamped," or provided with new feet. Ten yards of cloth are bought, and made into three coats, "a peticoat, a paire of briches, a paire of stokins," at a total cost, with "bottens threed and making," of £1.5s.4d. "Cloath to make James Cotha neckcloths" costs sixpence; his hat, shoes and stockings 5s.10d.; his suit of clothes 8s.4d.; his shirt and "linings" 1s.2d., his indentures as a parish apprentice 3s.4d.:— 17s.2d. in all for launching the little fellow out on life. Furze and Wood for poor folk costs 4s.6d. a load of 100 bundles. Some one is paid sixpence a week for tending Elizabeth Williams, who has fourteen pennyworth of victuals given her, and her house-rent (5s.) paid. A shilling is spent on mending the "ams hous oven," and there are various legal expenses—constables' charges, a warrant to distrain, a warrant to bring in new overseers, and so on. Altogether £27 odd is spent; and this was the normal amount for the first fifty years, though sometimes an unforeseen event disturbs the parish finances to an alarming extent. A pauper meets with an accident and has to have his leg amputated; the doctor charges ten pounds for the operation, and four guineas for curing the mortification that sets in afterwards: consequence—the poor rate goes up more than fifty per cent. Or a criminal appears on the scene; and what with catching him, and guarding him when caught, and taking him and the prosecutor to Bodmin, and attending the sessions, and facing the lawyer, and tipping the Bridewell keeper, the parish is over six pounds out of pocket. Towards the end of the eighteenth century expenses begin to leap up, until in 1813—the last year of the second volume—the "total disbosments" are more than £230, and a rate of 3s.4½d. has to be raised to meet them.

Nearly every page of these faded records reveals something of interest—some brief hint of drama, tragic or comic, or some curious detail of old-world life and manners. A few—only a few—of the most interesting entries may be given here.

In 1725 there is a series of items headed "The charges for poting William Penvose to the Hospetell at St Larans." The reader will realise the grim significance of this entry when he is reminded that St Lawrence's Hospital at Bodmin was a lezar-house. William Penvose was a Leper. The terrible disease seems to have lingered later in Cornwall than in other parts of the kingdom, but even in Cornwall it was practically extinct at this date, and Penvose must have been one of the last to be afflicted by it. The parish pays fees to "the docters for thare Jugment and the loyer for draing the setevecate," and six pounds "for inducting him into the Hospetell."[15] Then comes "For 8 Weekes dyet for him, 12s.0d.," and the rest is silence.

In 1691, in the midst of a number of commonplace entries, comes this startling one, like a blood-spot on the paper:

"Given to the men that went to take up the woman that laye dedde in the snow—and to two men that went to St Evall with the word that shee laye within thire parish . . . £0.02s.06d."

The tragedy is no sooner hinted at than it is relieved by the comically prompt measures that were taken to shoulder off this undesirable "find" on the next parish.

In 1711 died Elizabeth Pollard, who had for some years been receiving relief from the parish. Her burial expenses came to £1.2s.6d., and to defray these, the overseers had her goods sold. There is a memorandum in the book of the old lady's possessions—a pathetically scanty list:

> "One bed furnished; three bras pans; two bras Crokes; one tabell board; two chests; two pewter dishes; one cage; one curne; one pare of wool cards."

The old dame possessed no chair; she sat on her bed or on one of the chests, eking out her weekly dole by preparing wool for the spinners. Outside her door in the sunshine hung the cage with a goldfinch or perhaps a jackdaw in it. The "curne" was no other than a *quern*—the primitive hand-mill in which she ground her corn, as her prehistoric ancestors had done in their bee-hive huts. She baked her bread in one of the brass crocks, getting it on the hearth and raking the hot ashes over it, as housewives do in out-of-the-way parts of West Cornwall to this day. Her table was a rickety one; the trestles that supported the table-board were so far gone as not to be worth selling. Her pots and dishes were all of brass and pewter; for in those days earthenware was little known and less regarded in Cornwall.[16]

Elizabeth's goods fetched £1.10s. Thomas Nankivell, whose possessions were sold in the same way in 1723, had a larger stock. His bedstead and chest fetched 18s.6d., and he also owned a truckle bed, a rug, bolster, and sheets, and another "old decayed bed and boulster," beside looms, "styanes," or pipkins, trenchers, candlesticks, spoons, an "old Cobert," and various tools, s salt-cellar, and a "Mowse trap," (which fetched two-pence); and he even had "one old chair" to sit upon. The lot realised six pounds, which just paid Dr Lawrence's bill "for 16 Journeys attending Tho: Nankevell and Medicines."

One year the authorities resolve to revise the rate. They meet in conclave, and draw up—one can imagine with what pen-biting and head-scratching, especially over that tremendous word, *Majority*—the following urgent appeal:

> "Parishioners all
>
> This is to give you notis to bring a list of the names of every estate in your possesshion and The true yearly Vallu of each of them with out Screaning of your selves For that Shall be Deamed as Fraudelent And such Estate or Estates shall be Valued by there Neighbors And the Megoletre of the parish the Desine is for Makeing a Reguler and Just poor Rate And to bring it in Writeing with all speed to the Church Wardens or Over Seers of this your said parish."

Now and then the affairs of the great world beyond, with its wars and truces, send a ripple of excitement down this remote valley. In 1713 the parish expends eighteen-pence in celebrating the Peace of Utrecht. In later years public rejoicings are conducted on a less economical scale. The taking of Portobello—or "poartabelo," as the scribe has it—costs fifteen shillings "at John Whitfors and John Bulgers and Mary Cagas"—our three inns; and in 1748 £1.3s. was given the parishioners "to Drink his Majestics health on the Conclusion of the Peace" of Aix-la-Chappelle. Still later, the shadow of Napoleon strikes across us in the shape of numerous entries for Militia and Bounty money, and of enormously inflated prices for food and drink. In the black year of 1811 a peck of wheat costs us ten shillings—thrice its normal price.

At a poor person's burial the regular fees were a shilling each to the parson, the bedman (or sexton) and the ringers. Later, the sexton gets an advance of twopence, but "passon's" remuneration remains the same. In 1683 a "Regester Book" is bought for £1.11s., and next year "a paper book to record the names of those that ar buried," for fourpence. In 1763 we have this tantalising entry:

"Pd. for knowing Ann Bullings age— £00.00s.6d."

What was her age? Why did they want to know it? And how did they get the information for sixpence? On these points posterity is cruelly left in the dark. But there is no end to the picturesque and odd entries that might be quoted. "Travellers such is our polite name for tramps—are given threepence, and moved on to the next parish—"with horses," such is our eagerness to get rid of them. Mr Tregunna, our parson, turns an honest penny by selling us "Timber and Ire for the great Bridge," to the tune of £1.13s. We buy two hogsheads of pilchards and sell them to our poor at a loss; we spenc fivepence on the postage of a letter from Falmouth, and—it is census year—six shillings in "going Round the Parish taking the Nomber Parsons." We invest in yards and yards of Buckram, Dowlas, Linsey, Camblet, Everlasting, Swanskin, Tammy, and other obsolete stuffs. At one moment we are occupied with a payment for "duck to mend Henry Rundles Briches," at the next with a doctor's bill for mending Susanna Poyner's "Broken thy." We equip a rickety child with "leaders" at a cost of fourpence, and have whole families inoculated at five shillings a head. We dole out soap and candles, "trickle" and brandy, to old women in their sickness, thatch their roofs for them, mend their stays with "canves, boone, ynele, and threed," and allow them twopenn'worth of reeds to stuff their beds with. Once, and once only, we console an ailing pauper with some "trebaco." And once we perpetrate a bull: "Pd. our Expences Mitting Theoder Parkyn tho he neghleted" (neglected to come.)

Nearly every year poor children are fitted out and bound to parishioners, to learn "the art and mystery" of husbandry or housewifery. In one year—1800—eleven indentures are signed. Ratepayers were bound to take one or more of these children, in proportion to their wealth and standing in the parish; but it seems that sometimes they objected. Thus, in 1749, four parishioners—and one of them was Squire Willyams himself—are summoned before the justices "to shew cause why they would not take parish children apprentices." From nine to twelve years was the usual age of these children, and they were bound until they came of age, or (in the case of girls) till they should "contract mattrymoney." Some of them, no doubt, were kindly treated, but others led a hard life; people now living can remember the last of them, a grown man, working in the fields in tattered garments through which his knees and elbows showed. He ran away before his time was up, and was no more heard of.

The rich might move to and fro as they pleased in those days, but the law had something to say when a poor man wished to change his place of residence. The overseers naturally objected to the intrusion from other parishes of people who might, sooner or later, become chargeable upon them. So when, for example, in 1731, Francis Tom Tayler, and his wife moved from Little Colan to Mawgan, they had to bring with them a certificate from the Colan authorities, which promised to "provide for them in case either should become chargeable upon the parish of Mawgan." If no certificate was forthcoming, a running to and fro ensued; constables made journeys, declarations and depositions were taken before the justices, and finally comes an order to one parish to deliver over, and to the other parish to receive, So-and-so, who has not "gained a legal settlement in the said parish, nor produced any certificate." Occasionally there was a rough attempt to equalise the poor-rates; in 1827 Mawgan is mulcted in £45 for the relief of the poor of St Agnes.

In the earlier years the parish councillors numbered nine: the parson, and "the eight men of the parish"—four overseers, two churchwardens, and two "way-warns." About 1700 the number of the overseers dropped to three, and a few years later to two. In 1800 Mrs Jane Horsewell was elected; but the lady changed her mind, and did not serve. At first the way-wardens' bills were incorporated with the overseers'; and one can deduce the state of the roads from the lightness of their duties. At rare intervals appear such items as "For mending ye highway betwixt the bridg and the Churchtown £00.01s.00d." (1684); "Alowed Micharll Rindall for mending the wayes £00.04s.04d." (1696); "Paid for alle [*ale,* that is] for mending the highways £00.06s.10d." (1749)—a quaint way of putting it.[17] Their chief concern was with the bridges. In 1748 the rebuilding of "Churchtown Bridge" cost £6.5s.8d., including twenty-two shillings for "liquor." At the beginning of last century the road surveyors are promoted to an account book of their own, and expenses begin to mount up. In 1807 fifty pounds are spent; in 1824, £92. Next year there is a right-of-way dispute, with "expenses of Appealing against the Stoping of the rod," and the rate leaps up to £161. In 1830 it is £256, and a two-and-ninepenny rate has to be levied.

The names of these long-dead folk are interesting, as indeed names always are. In the matter of Christian names the men keep mostly to plain William, John, Richard, and the like, with and occasional Valentine or Hannibal, and once Trevennert—evidently a place-name; but the women are more graciously endowed. Here is a little list—an old-fashioned nosegay, that still smells sweet and blossoms in the dust. Font-names and surname go so prettily together, that we will not divorce them:

"Angelitt Budley, Aves Ellery, Vanety Tom, Abbigal Bennetta, Philippa Pascoe, Susanna Woon, Dolly Wilkin, Phebe Poyner, Thomasin Werry, Pascha Vanson, Ellonor Penvose, Sarah Rounsable, Jenefer Hicks."

Under the various disguises of Ouse, Osly, and Usle, we recognise what was once a common Cornish name, and should be so still; for was not St Ursula of Cologne a Cornish princess? The spelling of course varies wonderfully as times; Ceciley England's first name appears as Sesle, Sessle and Sesslee, and her second as Ingland, Inglet, and even Ingollet. William Jackandrew writes his old name now as one word and now as two. In 1762 we come across the name of Jane Arundell; if she came of gentle blood, it was to her shame, and profited her little, for she was then in receipt of parish relief. Her name is also spelt Arnold; and it is significant that the names Arnall and Rundall or Rindall—both suspiciously like Arundell—appear frequently in the earlier records. There is a touch of pathos when a poor deserted Hagar has her child baptized by the name of "Ismell."[18]

In the oldest document of all—the bond of 1623—appear the names of Otes George and Henry May, and the Georges and Mays still flourish in the parish. There are Jollys still as in 1637, and Cayzers as in 1684— one of the latter still rents the farm that his ancestors then occupied. But these, and a very few others, are the exceptions. Three fourths of the names that were most prevalent two hundred years ago have vanished; a like fate has overtaken both the substantial families—the Bennys, Berseys, Dungeys and Budleys—who held high office year after year, and signed their names with proud flourishes in the parish books, and the poor folk—Warmingtons, Morcumbs, Petricks, Minnows and Kites'—who scraped along on a shilling a day till the parish cart came to move them and their goods to the almshouse.

36

CARNANTON AND ITS WOODS

Little is known of the early history of the Manor of Carnanton. Perhaps it is the *Carneton* mentioned in Domesday; perhaps it is not. Later, it was in the possession of the Earls of Warwick; Sir Renfrey Arundell, father of the bishop, acted as their steward here in Henry VI's time. Their ultimate heiress was the Lady Anne Neville who was married to Edward Prince of Wales, and was afterwards wooed and won in such strange fashion by Richard Crookback. She conveyed Carnanton to the Crown and from the Crown it passed to the Father or grandfather of William Noye, Charles the First's famous—or, if you will, infamous—Attorney General.

Noye's story is well known; how at first he was foremost among the champions of the Parliamentary party, till Charles made him his chief law-officer, when he turned upon his former associates and rent them; how he led his king the first steps towards the scaffold by contriving the ship-money tax, and how his miserly heart was found after death to be shrivelled up into the semblance of a leather purse. It is interesting to note that one of the Five Members whom he was active in prosecuting was also connected with Mawgan. This was Denzell Hollis, whose font name is still the name of a farm in our parish; it was formerly a manor of the Denzells, whose heiress brought it to the Hollis family. Noye died in 1634, before the breaking of the storm he had conjured up. In his will he left £7.10s. to the poor of Mawgan, and most of his estates, including Carnanton, to his son Edward, "to be squandered, nor have I ever hoped any better." But Edward was killed two years later in a duel with the notorious Captain Byron, and Carnanton passed to his younger brother Humphrey, who is buried in Mawgan Church; and Humphrey's daughter, Bridgman Noye, brought it to John Willyams of Roseworthy, ancestor of its present possessors. The story goes that John Willyams was journeying to Oxford in 1685, when he was stopped at Exeter by the outbreak of Monmouth's rebellion; on his way back he stayed a few days with a St Columb friend, and there, "at some public exhibition," says the gossiping historian, he met Mistress Noye, fell in love with her, and married her very shortly after.

The Willyams family came originally from Stowford in Devon. Thomas Willyams, who died in 1566, was Speaker of the House of Commons; his cousin William settled in Cornwall, and had the manor of Roseworthy in Gwinear given him by Sir John Arundell in 1580. [One of William's sons, Roger, went to America, and founded, or helped to found, the plantations of Providence and Rhode Island.] The Rev. Cooper Willyams, great nephew of the first Squire of Carnanton, was chaplain of the *Swiftsure* at the Battle of the Nile, and published a description of the encounter. Two daughters of the house, Miss Jane Louisa Willyams and Miss Charlotte Champion Willyams, collaborated in a novel—"Coquetry"—which had the honour of being revised and corrected for the press by Sir Walter Scott. The former also wrote a history of the Waldensian Church, which was popular in the fifties. Colonel Brydges Willyams, eldest brother of the late squire, married an heiress of the Da Costas, a Jewish family of Spanish descent. This was the lady whose name is recorded in the life of Lord Beaconsfield, as having taken such a romantic interest in the fortunes of the greatest Jew of modern times. She died in 1863, and was buried in the family vault at Hughenden, leaving the greater part of her fortune to Disraeli, "in testimony of my affection and of my approbation and admiration of his efforts to vindicate the house of Israel." The late Mr Humphrey Willyams gathered at Carnanton a large collection of pictures, originals and copies of old masters; among them is a portrait of Handel by Sir Godfrey Kneller. It was to Mr Willyams that Mr Sewell Stokes dedicated his poem descriptive of the neighbourhood—"The Vale of Lanherne," a belated production of the Rogers and Campbell school, written in fluent and amiable, if undistinguished, Spenserian stanzas.

The present house at Carnanton is a Georgian building, replacing the Elizabethan mansion of Noye's time. Like every well-appointed country house, it has its ghosts and its spectral coach. But the chief glory of Carnanton is in its woods.

It is hard to conceive of the Lanherne valley as bare and treeless, yet so it must have been for many centuries. In ancient times, indeed, if the chronicles are to be trusted, a great forest overspread all Cornwall from the Tamar to Land's End. All through the tales of Celtic romance we walk beneath trees. Sir Tristram, the pride of Cornish Knighthood, was born in a Cornish wood, "under the umbre of a great tree," and he was the first to practice woodland arts in a knightly spirit. Those trees have long since gone up in smoke; King Arthur himself, according to Tennyson, began the work of destruction,

And felled

The forest, letting in the sun."

Carew, writing of Lanherne at the beginning of the seventeenth century, says that it was "appurtenanced with a large scape of land, which (while the owners there lived) was employed to frank hospitality; yet the same wanted wood, in lieu whereof they burned heath; and, generally, it is more regardable for profit then commendable for pleasure." By the overseers' accounts it appears that this fuel-famine continued well into the last century. Every year there are expenditures for "fuss" or "forze" for the use of the poor; and when a bridge or gate wanted mending, the wood must be fetched all the way from Padstow, the nearest sea-port.

Carnanton Woods, like most of our Cornish woods, sprang from that planting-fever—you may call it a Green Sickness—which seized on our ancestors in the eighteenth century, when, to mention no others, one Scottish laird set his fifty million of saplings. Successive owners of Carnanton have continued the good work—is there any which better deserves the gratitude of mankind?—until recent times. Even within living memory the slopes above the Lanherne entrance were still arable land.

One likes to think that the glamour of the Celtic woodlands was not altogether dissipated from the chimneys of mine and cottage, but sank into the soil and lay dormant, till the new roots struck down and drew it out again. At any rate, from whatever reason, whether of soil of climate or situation, our Cornish woods have a charm, an out-of-the-way beauty of their own. Nowhere do rooted creatures display a more wayward grace, a bolder eccentricity. The visitor who comes here in August or September sees them at their dullest time, though they are always lovely, from when the first leaf unfolds to when the last leaf falls. They are especially wonderful in early spring before a leaf appears, when the elms twigged with red coral, the ash-trees nibbed with black coral, the oaks with their horizontal branches overgrown with moss and fern, the larches covered with a livid efflorescence of blue-grey lichen, the dull sheen of the ivy that wreaths the trees and carpets the ground, and the amazingly bright glitter of the holly leaves, make up an unearthly vegetation, such as might wave in a league-deep sea.

At the entrance to the woods from the Mawgan end a company of fine beeches stands guard on the bank, their smooth trunks with countless inscriptions from the penknives of amorous rustics (for whom there is some excuse), and wanton tourists (for whom, begging their pardon, there in none). A little farther on, the drive passes through an avenue of elms, of the narrow-leaved variety peculiar to Cornwall. Anyone who is only acquainted with the hammer-headed, warty-limbed elms of the Midland hedgerows, will hardly recognise these slim beauties as their sisters. No excrescences disfigure their shapely stems, which shoot up, straight and slender and lightly plumed with twigs, to a height of thirty or forty feet before they fork and burst into a sheaf of foliage. Their proportions are scarcely stouter than those of a peacock's feather, which they resemble in outline. The least puff of air sets them rocking; in a gale they bend like whips, crossing heads. Their average height may be seventy or eighty feet; their girth, close to the ground, is often but three, or less.

Hereabouts, and elsewhere in the wood, are some very fine specimens of the Sycamore, that coast-loving tree which flourishes best where there is a whiff of salt in the air; and in the slopes to the right some savage dishevelled oaks survive from an earlier and wilder time. Farther on, the drive forks. The upper road leads past the house, and by open park-lands and shadowy avenues to the higher lodges on the St Columb road. The left-hand road dips into the valley, where the River (every stream large enough to float a moorhen is a river in Cornwall), bears it company for a while, prettily talking and dancing. The Royal, or Osmunda Fern flourishes in the marshy ground hereabouts, rising to a height of eight or nine feet, and easily overtopping the monstrous Lady Ferns and Broad Ferns that grow in its company. A little farther on, a gate to the left leads immediately to Lawrie's Mill, a favourite spot with picnic parties. The writer would be failing in his proper duty as a writer if he omitted to call this an idyllic spot. The white-washed cottage, the grey-roofed mill-house, the ruined mill-wheel, the weather beaten out-buildings, and the cliff of foliage behind, the hurrying stream before, the hills, gorse-clad or tree-clad, folding around, make up a scene which the artist might think too conventionally picturesque to endure putting on to canvas. One would not associate the place with commercial enterprise; yet old folk remember when a wool-stapler lived here and carried on a local manufacturing of blankets, and the air was tainted with the fumes of sulphur from the bleaching-shed, and one of the fields above (still known as Reek-Park) was white with blankets stretched to dry on their *recks*[6] or frames. There was no cart or carriage road here in those days. The miller's bags were conveyed to and fro by bridle-paths on horses and donkeys, whose backs were fitted with a long broad pad made of sheepskin stuffed with reeds.

Across the bridge, a noble ash-tree, eleven feet in girth, stands beside the stream, bending towards it, as a kindly old gentleman might bend and listen to the prattle of a child. Here is a rugged precipitous path leading to Higher Tolcarne, and worth scaling by those who have the breath to spare, for the sake of the exquisite view of the valley which unfolds as you climb. By continuing through Tolcarne hamlet and turning to the left, one may return to Mawgan by a pleasant upland road. The road behind the mill leads along the hillside, still overshadowed with trees, and bordered in spring with enormous primroses and anemones, in summer with regiments of six-foot foxgloves, to Nanskival—which in the old language means Woodcock Valley—the Carnanton dower-house.

The woods are crowded with wild life. The badger still haunts the slopes of Nanskival. Enormous numbers of wood-pigeons nest in the upper plantations; the green woodpecker is common, the great spotted woodpecker is sometimes seen, and magpies, jays, and wood-owls are more plentiful than is usual where pheasants are about. Of smaller birds, the smallest of all—the gold-crest—is especially numerous. You may fail to catch a glimpse of it—"that shadow of a bird," as White calls it—but you may hear its infinitesimal twitter all day long in the pines and larches. Of the summer migrants, chiff-chaff, willow-warbler, and blackcap nest here regularly, but the garden warbler and wood-wren seldom or never. One woodland bird, and that the most engaging of all—the nuthatch—is unaccountably absent from a spot that seems made for it.

The flowers would make a long catalogue. One can only mention two or three that grow in special profusion—the delicate Sanicle with its little round balls of grey blossom swinging on slender stalks; the Yellow Pimpernel that overgrows the less frequented paths; and the Ramsons, our most characteristic flower in mid-May, whose white stars are safely guarded from the gatherer of nosegays by their insufferable odour of garlic. Once the *Ramsay*, as it is called here, was a favourite pot-herb; and a native was heard to express his sympathy with the regrets of the Israelites over the flesh-pots of Egypt—glorious messes, as he pictured them, of beef and pork, "with a brave handful of Ramsay throwed in 'pon top."

THE CHURCHTOWN, AND OLD DAYS THERE

The stranger in Cornwall soon learns that every collection of houses, small or large, claims the title of *town* or *town-place*; so *Churchtown* explains itself. Mawgan Churchtown is divided into two district portions, known as "Up Street" and "Over-to-Shop"; the one extending up the hill in the direction of St Columb, the other—Penpont, "the head of the bridge," is its proper name—clustering about the ford over the leat or mill-conduit beyond the "great bridge." Central between the two, and facing the Church and the Convent, stands the Inn—once the "Gardener's Arms," now showing for its sign the crest and motto of the Willyams family—a Falcon, and the words in old Cornish, *Meor ras tha Dew,*—Great thanks to God.

Of the Falcon Inn, with its delightfully mingled atmosphere of rusticity and culture, its sanded floors and oak settles downstairs and its tastefully ordered and chosen books and pictures upstairs, much has been written. Associations with people of every condition cling about the place. Mrs Lynn Linton knew and loved it, and here Amy Levy, the poet of the London Plane-Tree, found a haven of brief rest just before her pathetic end. The south front is draped from the eaves to the ground in a luxuriant tangle of Passion Flower, that blooms even at Christmas, and about it all day the pigeons coo and flicker.

The late proprietor, Mr Samuel Gilbert, who died a few years ago at an advanced age, was one of the last of the old Mawgan worthies—a notable wrestler in his day, and a storehouse of old West-country songs. Two of the most charming in Mr Baring-Gould's "Garland of Country Song" were taken down from his lips. The old songs are dying out, in Mawgan as elsewhere, but there still remain a few elders who, when inspired with the proper modicum of ale, will lift their eyes to the ceiling, purge their faces of all sublimary expression, and pipe up some ancient ditty in the proper ancient style with tapping foot and quavering grace-note. When they go, the songs will go; for they are no more to be written down on paper than the blackbird's melody. Still at Christmas the carol-singers of the neighbouring parishes meet at the inn and "pitch" *Awake, Awake* or *Star of Bethlehem* in friendly rivalry before an audience of keen critics; and long may they continue to do so.

Many tales are told of the inn and its frequenters in the old days, when there was no law to close the doors at ten o'clock, and the topers would remain till five in the morning, drinking, wrestling and sleeping by turns. The week following Feasten Sunday was then one continual carouse. At these times, when a drinker was completely overcome, his companions would "make a mayor of him." A cart would be fetched from the stables, and one would hoist the victim inside, while another would get between the shafts, gallop off to the bridge, and tip his burden into the river.

Those were brave times, we are told, there was more going on in a week than there in now in a year. From the well-stored memories of the older folk, and from the account-books of the parish overseers (which go back to 1681), one can construct a curious picture of life as it was in a remote Cornish village during the eighteenth and early nineteenth century.

First one must sweep away the front part of the inn, and establish a second inn in the Lower House—the building that still stands adjacent to the school. The lych-gate disappears, and stocks and "hepping-stock" rise instead. On the hepping-stock, by which the farmers' wives alighted from their pillions, the sexton used to stand after service and give notice of farmers needing hands, lost property, litters of pigs for sale, and the like. The stocks stood by the Church gate, and have been used within the memory of man; the culprit was inducted into them before morning service on Sunday, and left there till the evening, with a crust and a jar of water to console him withal. In the parish accounts, under date of 1731, is entry:

"Expences about Setting James Ivey in the Stocks for his profaning the Sabbeth—11s.6d."

The last to suffer was one lately dead; his terrible crime was swearing at the parson and churchwardens at a vestry meeting. Another form of punishment for offences against clerical discipline was in force here until recent years. The offender had to bring to the Church-gate a cartload of bread—in a bad case it might be as much as £5 worth—and distribute it among the parishioners. Throwing the loaves was forbidden; each one must be duly handed out to a different applicant; but for all that, the distributor would get impatient at times, and the "box-hats" would begin to topple over as the loaves flew right and left through the crowd. Every man wore a tall hat in those days,[7] the rim of it worn away in front by the frequent application of finger and thumb, for a proper salute to the gentry was rigorously enforced. Poor folk lived hardly: wages through the eighteenth century remained fixed at 1s.2d. a day, and the nineteenth was far advanced before they rose much higher. Children were set to work almost as soon at they could toddle, and all the "little tagger" got was "twelve shillings a year and a lacing." The fare of a labouring family was "fish and taties one day, taties and fish the next, and a conger pie on Sunday." Sometimes it was poorer still. About April a farmer would lay in a "cave of turmuts" for the use of his labourers, cutting off the tops and storing the roots in an outhouse. One man hired himself to such a farmer, who fed him for the first fortnight on turnip pie, fried turnips, and boiled turnips, and for the rest of the month on a equally meagre diet of spinach and pepper-cress. At the end of the time he was asked if he would stay on for another month. "No, I don't think, master," was his reply. "I've been a fortnit in the house and a fortnit out to grass, and I reckon I'm fat enough to kill."

The family pig supplied a little variety occasionally but the tax on salt made bacon an expensive luxury; so when a pig was cut up, one joint would be reserved, and the others sent round among the neighbours, on the understanding that at future killings equivalent joints were to be sent in return. Trouble sometimes ensued.

But drink was cheap and plentiful. Most farmers brewed their March and October beer, and Mawgan was too near the coast for the supply of brandy to run short. In the eighteenth century the parish authorities "stood" drinks on every conceivable occasion; beer, or its equivalent peck of malt, at the christening of every pauper child, and brandy to the ringers and watchers at every pauper funeral; and every job about the roads or the alms house cost as much in liquor as in wages. Brandy then cost sixpence, or at most sevenpence a pint; in 1811 the price had risen to three shillings, and the palmy days of smuggling had begun. Fifty years ago, when there had been a successful "run" of liquor on the coast, men would come into the village with ox-bladders full of brandy, which they would hawk from door to door. The story is still told with great gusto, how the parish constable caught one of these illicit vendors and hauled him off before the squire. But on the way up to Carnanton, the man contrived to get out his penknife and cut a slit in the bladder. He got off, as it was not an indictable offence to carry a collapsed bladder about, even though it smelt of spirits.

They ploughed with oxen in those days. A full team consisted of eight animals, each of which had its allotted names and answered to it. "Spark and Beauty, Brisk and Lively, Neat and Comely, Goodluck and Speedwell" ran the pretty list. "While the hinds" says a traveller in 1808, "are driving these patient slaves along the furrows, they continually cheer them with conversation denoting approbation and pleasure. This encouragement is conveyed to them on a sort of chaunt, of very agreeable modulation, which, floating through the air from different distances, produces a striking effect both on the ear and the imagination." Much pride was taken in the team, and a man would plod half over the country on the report of an animal having been seen that exactly matched one of his own. Later, a mixed team of oxen and horse was employed, and at last the slow patient animals were discarded altogether. At an earlier period they were used as draught animals, yoked to a rough vehicle with

44

clumsy wheels, or even runners, which was called a butt, dray, or plow.[8]
The nine-foot goad has hardly yet gone out of use as a measure of land.
The long-handled shovel, with which the foot is of no help, is still in use—
a more graceful implement than the spade, to which Cornwall has never
taken kindly. There are odd names given to some of the farm tools.
What would an Essex labourer make of a *biddix* or a *visgey*?

Some old customs survive; some have only lately fallen into disuse.
One of the latter was the keeping of Paul's Pitcher Day. On the eve of
the feast of St Paul, the boys of the village went out after dark with all the
"sherds" or fragments of broken crockery they could lay their hands on,
and pelted the doors of unpopular inhabitants, crying—

> "Paul's eve,
> Give en a heave."

In the case of a particularly cantankerous householder, they would
first creep up and fasten the door with a cord. A similar observance,
known as Lent-Crocking, was once prevalent in Wilts and Dorset. The
ceremony of "making the hay sweet" is practised to this day. The maid
who ventures into a field of haymakers is captured and kissed, after her
cheek has been prepared for the salute by being vigorously rubbed with a
wisp of hay. A pretty ritual, though antiquaries trace it back to a horrible
origin: the laughing girl was once, they say, a human sacrifice to the
Earth Spirit, the kiss is to redeem her from the knife.

There are villages in West Cornwall where the inhabitants still
breathe a mediaeval atmosphere of prodigies, omens, and witchcraft;
at Mawgan, if any of the old superstitions are believed in, at any rate they
are little talked of, but the past generation was learned in charms and
mystical observances. One who was a small boy some fifty years ago can
just remember a funeral, where, after the coffin was lowered, there was a
nodding and whispering among the bystanders, and someone advanced
and cast a plaster into the grave: the wound from which it was taken being
expected to heal after this odd ceremony. In those days it was said that if
you ran nine times round a flat tombstone and then bent your ear to it,
you would "hear the dead sing." At a farm in the village is still preserved
a "kenning-stone"—a yellow marble of traslucent agate, which was used
to charm away kennings, or ulcers on the eye. To have its proper effect it
must be rubbed on the eyelid nine times for nine successive mornings,
fasting. It was considered unlucky to stand a bed crosswise to the floor-
boards; and a first consideration on looking over a new house was how to
arrange the beds so as to obviate this. One device to help a moribund
person to "die easy" was to turn the bed; another was to get Time out of
the way and clear the road for Eternity by stopping all the clocks in the
house. An old dame of the parish was a noted serpent-charmer. She

declared she could take an adder, set it on a board on the ground, and, by drawing a circle round it, prevent it from stirring till set of sun; but then her power ceased.

There is nothing of great interest in the village itself. Some way up the street on the right stand two cottages which were once the parish almshouses, and in that capacity figured in the old overseers' accounts. One would have thought that the aged paupers who dwelt there would have been constitutionally incapable of doing much damage to the structure; but something more than the usual fair wear and tear seems necessary to account for the perpetual tinkering that went on. Every year odd jobs are doing about the place, and every decade comes a grand expenditure for bushels of lime, loads of timber and stone, and thousands of "heling-stones" or roof-slates. These able-bodied veterans appear to have cherished particularly vindictive feelings against the lock that kept them in and the oven that cooked their pittance of food. Again and again such entries as these occur;

"Pd. a loke for the alms hows puten up, 8d."
"Pd. for an Oven for ye poor, 7s.6d."
"Pd. for helping ye Oven home and attendance for putting Inn Oven, 1s.6d."[9]

Nearly opposite to those cottages is the old Bowling Green, once the focus of the fair which used to be held here on Midsummer Day. Two fields behind the Green are known as Castle Fields; here, perhaps, once stood that "Castle Fust in Carnanton," which was already in ruins when William of Worcester made his tour of Cornwall in 1478.

In the opposite direction a pleasant brief stroll may be taken, crossing the bridge—"the Great Bridg" of the old accounts, and going up through Penpont, where the Methodists—not so all-powerful in North Cornwall as elsewhere in the Duchy—have a Chapel. Here is a bit of street which reminds me of the villages farther west—close-huddled houses with whitewashed portals, window-sills adorned with spar-stones, and little gardens gay with old-fashioned flowers. A little way beyond the road forks; hereabouts, in a recess in the rocky bank, was the place where the oxen were shoed, or *cued*. The right-hand road leads up a steep ascent; and if as you climb you are disposed to be out of humour with these perpetual hills—"high churlish hills," as an old traveller calls them—you may like to be reminded of the ingenious consideration by which Carew turns aside this reproach of ruggedness from his native county. Perhaps it *is* hilly; but you must remember the consequent saving of space. "If you match it with other champaign shires, methinks, I may gather the same to be better inhabited, within a like circuit of miles, because the plenty of hills and valleys afford a larger quantity of ground thereto."

This particular hill is commendably brief. The road soon dips into a hollow, where you will find a farm-Lanvean, "the little enclosure"—a picturesque thatched and whitewashed cottage gleaming against a background of tall elms, and (as often as not) a lady-artist intently sketching the same. Below is a gate through which a steep path descends into the village again. The Rectory stands high on the left, an uncompromisingly Gothic building for which Mr Butterfield is responsible. The old Parsonage stood lower down—an Elizabethan house, "very picturesque and exceedingly inconvenient," writes one who spent his childhood there.

"Like the one-eyed calendar in the 'Arabian Nights,' people who came to see us generally went on opening doors till they lighted on the corner of the house where we burrowed. But it was pleasant home nevertheless, with the deep porch and its two stone seats; the windows embowered in clematis and Indian rose bushes, the trim gardens with their beehives, and walks bordered with-box; two or three pools, dignified with the name of ponds; and—pride and glory of all—the long grassy walk shaded with filberts." *Autobiography of a Cornish Rector.*

The stone hedges here are overgrown with the graceful Ivy-leaved Toadflax, and that most singular of wayside plants, the Wall Pennywort. "Penny-cakes," the Mawgan children call it, from its circular leaves, which range in size from that of a tea-saucer to that of a silver penny. Its spikes of yellow-green curl out of the crevices and stand bolt upright against the wall; in winter they shrivel, but remain without falling till spring, each little brown mummy erect in its niche.

A few words may be added concerning the people of to-day. If a line be drawn down the Cornish coast from Morwenstowe to Sennen, Mawgan will be found to be almost exactly on the point of bisection. Here is a key to the understanding of Mawgan folk, their speech and ways. Saxon stolidity and Celtic vivacity meet in equipoise, and the result is and excellent mixture. Less imaginative than the fisher-folk of the West, they are for that reason more truthful and trustworthy. They have their share of Celtic wit, and they do not lack the more blessed Saxon gift of humour. "Yokel" would be the last word to apply to the North Cornish farm-hand. Their speech—the speech of the mid-Duchy is so free from provincialisms that it hardly deserves to be called a dialect. A few words and grammatical peculiarities that were (most of them) good book-English in Shakespeare's time,[10] a preference for the broad *a* sound in such words as *sea* and *meat,* and the faintest touch of the Devon brogue in the occasional substitution of *v* for *f,* make up the chief sum of their vernacular peculiarities. Some pretty and interesting old words are in use.The flexible basket used by carpenters is still called a *frail;* in the

Genevan Bible of 1560, Abigail presents David with "a hundred frailles of raisins." Hawthorn berries are *aglets*—a Shakesperian word.*Wallop* for "gallop" is found in Mallory. *Country,* as elsewhere in Cornwall, is used as equivalent to Mother Earth; a house with the hill-side rising steeply behind it is said to be "built up against the country." *Leisurable,*‡ "at leisure," might well be adopted into literary English. *Guff* is an expressive word for worthless rubbish, and *gamut* for any kind of lively diversion. Donkeys do not bray here, nor do they "bleat," as in South Cornwall; they *hoot.* Instead of whining, dogs *creen*; and badgers *grizzle,* geese *gabble,* and hens *cockle.*[11] All Cornishmen love the symbols of speech, and the talk of Mawgan blossoms with similes, metaphors, and gnomic utterances. Ripening corn is "as yellow as a kit's foot"—a quaint likeness, fetched from afar. A paltry wayside inn is "tied to the hedge with a bremble;" a husband who is a "good fellow out, and a brute home" is said to "hang his fiddle outside the door;" and on the other side of the matrimonial equation we have—

> " A smoking house and a scolding wife which descends from mediaeval times. Better a poor fellow were dead than alive."

Mawgan loves a good story well told. We have in the parish some past masters in the art of dramatic narration, and to hear one of these tell a favourite yarn is a sheer delight, so nicely calculated is every effect, so richly humorous every phrase. And a hundred merry japes are current, that might have come straight out of an Elizabethan jest-book. Such is the tale of the man "up Camelford way" (it is never a man down Mawgan way), who wished all the world were dead, except himself and his mother; then he would go on farming, and mother would keep a public-house; of the domestic squabble, where the husband, finding himself on the floor and his wife vigorously kicking him, protested—"Be a man, Mary Ann, be a man;" of the folk down Falmouth way, who were discovered attempting to hoist a cow on the roof of a house, that she might clear off the "ivies" growing there; and of the first advent of a four-wheeled vehicle in a certain mining town, when an excited crowd followed it about, cheering the gallant little front wheels, and holding their breath when, as a corner was turned, the big wheels threatened to catch them up and run them over. Of the subtle form of humour which is imperceptible to the perpetrator, one randam example out of many must suffice. An old lady of the parish took great pride in her hair, which she was accustomed to anoint profusely with castor oil till it shone again. Once something happened to ruffle her dignity, and a friend attempted to soothe her with soft flattering words.

"How beautifully glossy your hair is, Mrs X—," said the peace-maker.

48

"Ess," replied the old lady, drawing herself up. " 'Tis written in Scripture that the righteous shall shine."

THE RIVER VALLEY

Our river rises in the moorlands, behind the legendary Castle-an-Dinas, where King Arthur had a hunting-box, and close to the birth-place of its bigger sister, the Fal. It enters the parish by way of the woods, and runs a gay course down to the village, now rushing headlong over a weir, now loitering in deep pools under the trees, fed by the way by fifty lesser nymphs that

"on side of hills
From plaything urns pour down the rills,"

Beyond the village it proceeds more sedately through a series of "moors," as the marshy seaward meadows are called here, till it quietly slides into the Atlantic over the wide sands of Mawgan Porth, a mile and a half below the Churchtown. Mellanhayle is its appropriately musical name, derived from two old Cornish words signifying Mill on the River. Its companion stream, which runs down the adjoining valley and meets it near the sea, has no fixed name, but is called at different points by the names of its fords—Whitewater, Belingey Water, Trevedras Water, and so on. Each of the sisters has her own characteristic temper, we are told; under the influence of a "suant shower," the higher stream, choleric but easily placated, will be up in flood and down again before the slower and more enduring rage of Mellanhayle has fully risen. Both swarm with mountain trout, small but toothsome. About the middle of July, the salmon peal begin to come up the larger stream, and are caught at night by men wading with nets. The brief season ends at the beginning of September, the fish on their return to the sea in March being in the poorest condition, and not worth catching. The "scourers," or young peal, are later in departing, according to the local rhyme:

"First week in May
The scourers go to say."

Several pairs of that most interesting of water-birds, the Dipper, divide the river between them, each couple keeping rigidly to its own preserve of a quarter-mile or so; and this is one of the breeding haunts of the prettily-clad Grey Wagtail, which is with us summer and winter. Herons haunt the valley all the year round; and geese, teal, mallards, and other wild-fowl, with snipe and jack-snipe (called here "fool-snipe"), frequent the flooded marshes in winter.[12] From May to August the moors are gay with flowers. First come the King-cups, spreading in great sheets of cloth of gold, and among them grows the delicate Buckbean with its shining triple leaf and its spike of pale pink blossoms. In June the Iris reigns supreme; and in the following month the flowers are beyond counting. There is a secluded meadow by the higher stream, where no cattle ever set foot, and the grass grows high, and innumerable flowers shine through its translucent green atmosphere—"beautiful and peaceful tribes" of Meadow-sweet, Valerian, Forget-me-not, Ragged Robin, Water Bedstraw, Marsh Orchis, and others. The Bog Pimpernel nestles with shut eyes in beds of sphagnum, and in the midst rise great clumps of the Osmunda Fern with its curious brown spore-clusters.

There are two or three ways for pedestrians down the valley, and the visitor with time to spare should go at least a short distance along one of them. You may start from where the road forks above Penpont, and take the cart-track that diverges through a gate to the left. The view within is charming. On the left the church and convent appear among their trees; to the right the seaward hills fold together in curves that are a delight to the eye; below is the "Long Moor" (where some bronze celts and a bronze sword were dug up in 1812), and along its verge the river winds and gleams under the overhanging boughs of the Nuns' Grove. The slope on which you stand is a favourite haunt of Jack-o'-Lantern in autumn nights. The path continues along the hillside, past Winsor Mill, through corn-fields and furzy crofts, till it comes out into the parish road just above Gluvian Farm. Looking across the valley hereabouts, you will notice a row of elms that have banded themselves together for mutual protection against the north-westerly gales. The first—the nearest to the sea, crouches low, its boughs on the exposed side almost touching the ground; the next lifts its head a little higher, the third a little higher yet, and so on, until the last few are enabled to rise to their full stature. The tops of the boughs from end to end form a continuous shelving line—a penthouse on which the wind strikes obliquely and glances off. In a combe close by there is a wych-elm that began life as a seedling on the side of a low hedge, and has never had the courage to rise above it; it is full-grown, and a curious spectacle it makes, with its great trunk stretching out in a horizontal line over a marshy hollow. Even on calm days, what a strain must there be on the roots!—a fifty-fold strain that never relaxes, for their task is not simply to balance and anchor the trunk, but to hold the whole enormous mass at arms' length, as it were.

At the end of the foot-path a choice of ways is offered. If you are for the beach, you may continue on the road, through Gluvian, (the *Glivian Flamank* of the old records), and so over the little hill beyond to a sight of the sea. In a field to the left of the road stand the ruins of an ancient chapel, now used as a barn. Or you may take the steep lane opposite the end of the footpath, cross the ford called Pollycarn, and make for the sea by way of the meadow denominated Church Close, which has its history, and its fiction; for the right-of-way across it was once the subject of a fierce dispute between two farmers, and out of the dispute Mr Baring Gould fashioned a novel. Or again you may make your way back to the Churchtown by turning to the left out of Gluvian farm-yard, crossing the moors, and climbing up the other side of the valley to Tolcarne Merock, where a grey farm-house shelters behind a screen of lofty elms. Thence you return by a shady lane through Polgreen, once a gentleman's residence, and past the Nuns' Grove into the village.

THE COAST, AND OUTLYING PARTS

For weeks of winter nights together the low continuous roar of the sea sounds in the ears of Mawgan; but Mawgan has little concern with it. If we were on the south coast there would be a fishing settlement in the cove, and pigs and pilchards would mingle in the talk round firesides; but on this inhospitable shore there are no boats, and the Churchtown is a thoroughly inland village, though barely a mile and a half from the tidal limit. Gulls hover over the valley in rough weather, or follow the ploughman in assiduous crowds; farm carts go down to the beach to gather sand for manure, and sometimes a pleasure-party will make an excursion to pick mussels from the rocks; but these are our only links with the ocean.

The coast line of the parish extends from the bottom of Tregurrian Valley, where a brand-new hotel affronts the Atlantic, to the southern limit of Bedruthan Sands—about three miles of cliffs and sandy beaches; pleasant to ramble over in fine summer weather, but in winter a besieged rampart, battered for weeks on end by furious gales and surges. A wild coast, with traditions of wild doings. The Rev. John Tregenna, Rector of Mawgan, who died in 1754, founded a charity which is still administered, and from the benefits of which *wreckers* are expressly debarred; and it may be whispered that the old spirit in a mitigated form is not yet extinct. There are old men dwelling in the two coastward hamlets of Tregurrian and Trevarrian, who still have the reputation of being "terrible wrecking chaps;" but their wrecking takes the comparatively harmless—and even, according to Cornish notions, laudable—shape of circumventing the coastguardsmen in the matter of such stray goods and bits of timber as may be floated ashore after a storm. Tales are told—but they are told in confidence, with a wink and a grin, and they shall not be repeated here. However, there is no harm in retailing one old reminscence of the fifties: how many bales of silk once came ashore from a wreck near Bedruthan; how the folk of all the neighbouring parishes from St Merryn to St Columb Minor flocked to the spot, men, women and children; and how the women slipped off their crinolines, and stood while the men wound yards and yards of silk about their bodies. Pieces of that selfsame silk are preserved in some of the farmhouses to this day.

Smuggling, too, was rife; but as a rule the men of Mawgan parish took only a subsidiary part in it. The "venturers"—as the runners of the cargo were called—came over on their horses and donkeys from the mining districts about Roche and St Dennis, and the Tregurrian and Trevarrian folk merely acted as their guides along the by-paths. Beacon

Cove, a solitary little bay below Trevarrian, was the favourite landing-place; there was a tin mine here, the shafts and adits of which are still to be seen, where the "kegs" were stored against a convenient time for removal. Stories are told of fierce encounters, when the venturers leapt from their horses and plied their big whips on the backs of the preventive men till they fled howling. The regular trade ended in a mishap. The cargo was to have been landed as usual in Beacon Cove, but the weather was unfavourable, so the crew sank the kegs off-shore, and put into Newquay. A storm came on; the barrels broke loose from their moorings, and floated in on the tide. "Gov'ment" woke up, rubbed its eyes at the sight, and shut the stable door by establishing a preventive station at Mawgan Porth.

There are some interesting caverns along this coast. A small one, not far behind the Watergate Hotel, is pierced in the metalliferous rock, and the walls of it are a gorgeous sight when the evening sun shines in— all painted and enamelled with streaks and patches of emerald green and peacock blue and every shade of orange and gold. On the north side of Mawgan Porth, far down, and only accessible at low tides, is a particularly fine cave, deep and lofty, with a magnificent natural archway at its entrance. At Livelow, on the Watergate side of Beacon Cove, may be traced the relics of one of those cliff-castles which once guarded the Duchy's "long naked sides" (as Carew calls them), from Tintagel to Cape Cornwall.

There runs along the northern cliff of Mawgan Porth a curious sunken way, with a ramport of earth on the seaward side, which might at a first glance be taken for the remains of a similar ancient fortification. But it is nothing of the sort; and thereby hangs a tale of the maddest enterprise that ever Cornishman undertook. In the latter half of the eighteenth century, there lived at St Columb a Mr John Edyvean, a blind gentleman of some property and some talent. Being struck with the waste of time and labour incurred by the farmers of the district in carting the oreweed and sand, which was their favourite manure, up from the sea, be cast about him for means to facilitate the business. Those were the days of the great Duke of Bridgewater, when engineers were busy covering Britain with a network of waterways. Why not a canal? The idea might have occurred to any other man only to be dismissed as impracticable in a district of rolling hills and deep ravines. But the blind man brooded on it in darkness, till it became a fixed idea; and a fixed idea with capital behind it will move mountains. In 1773 he obtained an Act of Parliament for making a canal which was to run in a semicircular direction from Mawgan Porth, round by St Columb Major, and so back to the sea at St Columb Porth. He began to dig and bank, and actually completed the canal—without locks, be it remembered—as far as Whitewater on the north-eastern border of Mawgan parish. Barges were floated on it, and manure was loaded in them; but by this time the projector had spent all his own money and most of his sister's, and he found that he was not likely to re-establish his fortunes by the portage of manure through a thinly populated district. Besides, the scheme had one fatal defect: it literally would not hold water. No attempt was made to puddle the channel, and the sides, of light, porous soil, leaked grievously. The poor man died soon after, of a broken heart, it is said; but the canal may still be traced for some miles—a forlorn ditch bemazed among hills, twisting wildly round abrupt curves, desperately banking itself up on slopes, here converted into a cart-road, there into a duck-pond, and coming to a sudden end on the verge of the cliff, fifty vertical yards above the sea—a proper place for suicide. Here may be seen the oblong shaft which was sunk through the rock into a cavern below, and through which the sand was raised in baskets and tipped into the barges. In the cuttings of the canal grow the finest blackberries in the district, so it was not dug altogether in vain. But of such stuff the nightmares of civil engineers are made.

Kestrels and ravens nest on the cliffs with the gulls and shags and jackdaws. Now and then that noblest of hawks, the Peregrine Falcon, is seen, and the Cornish Chough is occasionally found in the neighbourhood of Livelow Head, which is also one of the few Cornish breeding-places of the Oyster Catcher. Seals are seen once in a way. The Samphire, Sea-pink, Sea Campion, and Danish Scurvy-grass grow profusely where-ever they can find a hold for their roots, and the short grass of the cliff-tops is thickly starred in summer with countless sea-loving plants. Sun and salt wind[14] rule together here, and the result is a kind of stunted luxuriance. The plants flourish discreetly; they have scarcely lifted their heads above the soil before they hasten about their affairs of blossom and seed. The heather and gorse grow in thick spherical masses, not one twig daring to lift itself above its fellows; in their dense clumps the Milkwort, Lady's Bedstraw, and Burnet Rose nestle for protection; Eyebright and Centaury are sturdy dwarfs; and the lovely Vernal Squill hardly ventures on the luxury of a stalk at all, but flowers straight from the ground. It is charming so—a little sudden fancy of the earth. There is a piece of barren ground on the way to Bedruthan that in June and July is clotted all over with the pretty English Stonecrop, its white flowers tinged with delicate pink. The Kidney Vetch or Lady Fingers is as capricious in its colouring as elsewhere along this coast, running up the gamut of colour from white through cream and yellow and orange to crimson and even purple.

The *townas* or sand-hills at Mawgan Porth are a little world to themselves, with their own flowers and birds. Here, on the pale yellow sand, among the pale blue-green rushes, the Mullein lifts its tall spike, and the tiny Sea Storksbill spreads over the ground; the unattractive Hound's Tongue is the most plentiful weed, and you may chance to come across the sinister Henbane, with its yellow flowers marked with brownish purple stains. "A devilish plant," said a lady visitor. Linnets wheel about in twittering flocks, the Wheatear runs from hillock to hillock, and the smart little Stonechat perches and sings on the extreme tip of a bramble-spray. Hereabouts are some hedges of Tamarisk—a scrubby unattractive shrub for three parts of the year, a vision of beauty when it puts forth its pink tasselled flowers. No good Cornishman will refuse to believe the tradition that the Duchy owes three things to the ancient Phoenicians, of which the Tamarisk is one, and the other two are clotted cream and saffron cake.

The famous rocks of Bedruthan are in St Eval parish, beyond our survey; but it may be noted here that not everybody is of one mind as to their grandeur and interest. Not long ago a party of country folk from the china-clay district drove across to visit them. They stopped at Mawgan on their way back, and were asked what they thought of Bedruthan. They didn't think anything of Bedruthan—nothing but a parcel of old rocks. Next time they took an outing they were going to a "say-poort," where there was something going on, and something could be had to eat—and to drink.

The north-eastern portion of the parish is occupied by a spur of the great range of barren uplands that form the backbone of Cornwall. Here, at the spot called Sparable Point on Denzell Downs, is the highest ground in the parish. From the top a fine view is to had, embracing the coast from Pentire right down to Cape Cornwall, the valley of the Camel, the far-off peaks of Brown Willy and Rough Tor, and the wild tumbled country about St Dennis and Hensbarrow. There are some ancient remains here—two or three sepulchral mounds, and traces of an entrench-ment marking the site of a hill-top village. The Sweet Gale (locally called Goyle) grows plentifully in the marshy bottoms, together with Cotton Grass, Sundew, and other moisture-loving plants. Denzell has already been mentioned as the name-place of Charles I's playfellow, Denzell Hollis. The last of the old proprietors was one John Denzell, a sergeant-at-law of Henry VIII's time, who died in 1533. Hals speaks of a free chapel attached to the manor, the "rubbish and down-fallen walls" of which were still to be seen in his time, though now they have entirely disappeared. There is one remarkable thing about the farm-house here, which must not be passed over. A certain room in it is said to be haunted by the ghost of a man with a wooden leg, or rather by the ghost of the wooden leg itself, which at the appointed hour of night comes stumping in, seeking, one presumes, for the body to which it was attached in life— if one can speak of life in connection with a timber toe.

The rest of the parish, pleasant as it is to ramble over by road and foot-path, offers little to detain the minutest historian. It is well accidented, as the French say, with hill and valley, pasture, corn-land and heathery waste, and dotted over with snug farms and tenements; but it has no outstanding features to attract the casual eye. It is typically Cornish, but Cornwall does not flaunt her charms in the face of every newcomer. To some she never reveals them at all; Stevenson could see nothing in her, just as he could make nothing of her people. The unique charm of Cornwall is a matter of delicate differences. There is a touch— just a touch—of strangeness in everything. The hedgerow flowers are a little bigger, their colours are a little brighter, rarities are common, and many that are common elsewhere are here conspicuously absent. The trees grow a little differently. The smell in the air is not quite the same. The contour of the land, the way the hills fold on one another, the turns the valleys take, will seem just slightly unfamiliar to the observant stranger; but as a rule there will be no violent appeal to your admiration. Cornwall woos gently, and you must meet her half-way; but to love her once is to love her for ever. Nowhere can you learn the lesson more agreeably than here at Mawgan. In the words of the local bard:

"You may search in and out, you may hunt up and down,
But you won't find an equal to Mawgan Churchtown:
Lanvean and Polgreen and Tolcarne and Trevedras,
Lanherne and Nanskival and Gluvian and Deerpark,
Trevarrian, Tregurran, Trevena, Carloggas, Trenoon and Bolingey and Mawgan Churchtown."

FOOTNOTES . . .

1. So Hollinshead; but according to other accounts it was a later Sir John who owned a gold suit for every week in the year, and the Arundell who was drowned was not the general, but an eminent pirate.

2. In 1746 Lanherne was rated to "The Honoble Henry Arundell Esq. and Lady Gifford."

3. The Vyvyan Horse and the Coleshill Goat also occur, and the three Roundels on a Bend of the Whitleigh family.

4. The old vestry was put to odd uses at times. In 1687 the overseers paid 11s.2d. "for Cleeving of Woode for the Poore, for Makeing the Wagges [wedges] and Carring it in to the Vestrey."

5. Hullah's Psalter was used in the fifties and sixties. Before that, the singers had M.S. volumes of tunes, handed down from father to son, and added to from time to time. They were arranged for three parts in the proper ancient way—air in the tenor, and harmony supplied by treble and bass.

6. i.e. *racks* Cf. Overbury's Character of a Creditor. "Every term he sets up a tenters in Westminster Hall, upon which he racks and stretches gentlemen like English broadcloth beyond the staple of the wool."

7. And a fustian coat. Black was the sign of gentility, and the most prosperous yeoman would not think of wearing it. A new suit was worn to church for a year; then it served to go to market in for another year; then it descended to everyday use, and lasted till the scarecrow required a new outfit.

8. "Most of the traffic, such as it was, was carried on by means of long strings of mules, which crawled in single file up and down the mountain paths, as they still do in Spain. Often and often of a still night have I listened to the tinkling of their bells, and the wild song of the *arrieros,* as they wound through our valley." *Autobiography of a Cornish Rector.*

9. 1688, Pd. Mr Hayman for carring Margret Georges fuell and goods unto the alms house, 1s.6d. Pd. Trevena Kessel to set up Margret Georgs bedsteed and righting him, 6d." 1719, "Pd. Henry Larans for making the Almas House garn hage [garden hedge], 1s." 1747, "Pd. for spleting of a oak board for the parish house, 3d." 1759, "Pd. for mending ye parish Bed, 7d."

10. For example, the use of *to-night,* = either last night or next night, according to the time of day. So Romeo—"I dreamed a dream and to-night." The common use of *terrible* as an adverbial intensive—"Seeming to me, the old cow edn' looking so terrible well"—is found in North's Plutarch: "But the snow was so deep, the cold so terrible sharp."

11. If the *mot juste* is not found ready to hand, it may be invented. "Once," an old lady is reported to have said, "I had the prettiest cage of teeth in the parish; but I took so much doctor's trade [medicine], that it *solivated* 'em, and I lost four at a stroke. But I take God to witness," she added, "that I never put a toothbrush to them in my life."

12. A Golden Eagle and a Spotted Eagle were shot here in 1861, and in 1884 the only Cream-coloured Courser that ever ventured into Cornwall. The somewhat rare and extremely local Cirl Bunting nests in the valley in considerable numbers. The Hoopoe pays us an occasional visit.

13. Every field and enclosure in the parish has its name; sometimes its name and its nickname besides. The Celt has a genius for nomenclature. Bannister's *Glossary* contains some 20,000 Cornish place-names, and the list is far from complete.

14. With nibbling rabbits for its allies.

15. He may have come of gentle stock. The name of Willam "Penvose gent," appears in a bond of 1637. Penvose is the name of a farm in the parish.

16. Cornwall, as the head-quarters of the tin-trade, was then a chief seat of the pewter manufacture, and was naturally ill-disposed towards the new-fangled "clome." "At the first introduction of earthenware," we read, "it was a popular cry to destroy the clome and bring back the use of tin."

17. One year (1723) they venture on an experiment, which must have turned out unsatisfactorily, since it was never repeated. "Payed the paver for making 175 yards of pavement at 2 penc the yard £01.09s.02d."

18. Among the miscellaneous papers is a remarkable magistrates' order having reference to this child. It was made "at St Collumb the 18th daye of November Ano Dmi 1641 by Samuell Cosowarth and John Carter Esqrs," and sets forth that at the time the child was borne, John Bennett and Henry Morcomb, "who weere then Cunstabells of the said pishe of Maugan," neglected to make proper inquiries into the matter, so that the child was likely to become a burden to the parish; so the said constables are ordered to take the said child from the said parish and maintain it at their own costs, "and this our Order to stand Untill wee shall see good cause to the contrary."

61